RECENT JAPANESE STUDIES of MODERN CHINESE HISTORY (II)

RECENT JAPANESE STUDIES of MODERN CHINESE HISTORY(II)

Translations from Shigaku zasshi for 1983-1986

Joshua A. Fogel

M. E. Sharpe, Inc.
ARMONK, NEW YORK
LONDON, ENGLAND

Copyright © 1989 by M. E. Sharpe, Inc.

Available in the United Kingdom and Europe from M. E. Sharpe, Publishers, 3 Henrietta Street, London WC2E 8LU.

Published simultaneously as Vol. 22, No. 1-2 of *Chinese Studies in History*.

Library of Congress Cataloging-in-Publication Data

Recent studies of modern Chinese history : translations from Shigaku zasshi for 1983–1986 / by Joshua A. Fogel.
    p.   cm.
   Includes bibliography.
   ISBN 0-87332-564-8
   1. China—History—Ming dynasty, 1368–1644—Bibliography.
  2. China—History—Ch'ing dynasty, 1644–1912—Bibliography.
  3. China—History—20th century—Bibliography.   I. Fogel, Joshua
A., 1950– .   II. Shigaku zasshi.
  Z3108.A3R4   1989
  [DS735]   88-37051
  016.951—dc19   CIP

Printed in the United States of America

Contents

RECENT JAPANESE STUDIES of MODERN CHINESE HISTORY(II)

JOSHUA A. FOGEL

Introduction

The texts that follow originally appeared in Japanese in the scholarly journal *Shigaku zasshi*, the oldest historical journal in Japan which this year celebrates its centenary. Each year this journal devotes its May issue to surveys of the previous year's historical research in Japan on all areas of the world. I have translated here two sections from each May issue (for 1983-1986) covering: Ming and Qing China; and the post-Opium War period.

This periodization deserves a brief comment. While earlier Chinese history is periodized according to dynasties for the summaries in each May issue of *Shigaku zasshi*, when the editors arrive at the 19th century, their methodological tools shift radically in what appears to be an enormous mixed metaphor. Where the rise and fall of imperial houses is sufficient to allocate responsibility in these summaries before the Opium War, that event still garners sufficient importance to be worthy of a periodization point. Furthermore, it earns the non-dynastic title in *Shigaku zasshi* of "Modern" (*Kindai*). This period runs through the 1911 Revolution and into the early Republican period, roughly to the May Fourth Movement. Subsequent events (May Fourth to the present) fall into a period entitled "Contemporary" (*Gendai*). The modern-contemporary periodization still reflects the influence of the People's Republic of China where the Opium War and the May Fourth Movement are still accorded such significance.

This view would once have signified a conscious stand in favor of the momentous importance of the Opium War, the intrusion of Western capital into China, and the destruction of the hitherto natural Chinese economy, as well as the subsequent introduction of "bourgeois-democratic" ideas in the May Fourth period. Nowadays, few Japanese scholars can get too excited about the old Tokyo-Kyoto debate over when modern Chinese history really began. The *Shigaku zasshi* periodization is a lingering remnant from an older time.

As the reader will soon see, much more interesting subjects are being debated among Japanese Sinologists. Research on Chinese society, economic institutions, and particularly agriculture continues to attract considerable attention in Japan. A number of fascinating essays appeared over the past few years which have linked legal history with agricultural history. Rebellion and the role of religion in it also continue to exert a forceful influence among Japanese scholars. Even intellectual history, traditionally not the strongest suit in Japanese Sinology, has clearly made some important gains, although the "modern" period appears to be the principal beneficiary of this development.

One significant development is the appearance of more studies in the field of Chinese women's history. This was not an altogether ignored field in Japan before 1983, but it was virtually ignored in the *Shigaku zasshi* summaries. Three of the ten authors of the essays that follow are women, and that fact may help explain the increased attention focused on women's history in China. As in the United States, however, Japanese research on Chinese women's history tends almost exclusively to concern the 20th century. What we have in both countries is more on the order of a history of women in the Chinese revolution, rather than the history of women in China. The latter will surely follow on both sides of the Pacific.

The saddest non-development over the past decade is the apparent fact that Western scholars have not increasingly developed an appreciation for the enormous contribution of our Japanese colleagues. At least, that appreciation has not led to a concerted effort to learn and use Japanese materials more than in the past. It is still possible to earn a Ph.D. at many institutions of higher learning without adequate coverage of the Japanese materials in one's sub-field, and it is still possible to have one's work published with the same glaring lacunae. The aim of these translations was to foster such an appreciation and serve as a tool for Western scholars dumbfounded as they stood before an inestimably large volume of Japanese writings on virtually every area of Chinese history. Perhaps it may yet have a latent effect.

The odd-numbered chapters that follow on Ming-Qing history first appeared in *Late Imperial China*, the reincarnation of *Ch'ing-shih wen-t'i*. I would like to thank Charlotte Furth, co-editor of *Late Imperial China*, for the enormous help she offered in editing these chapters and even some of the ones on "modern" (post-Opium War) China. Those latter chapters, the even-numbered ones, appeared first in *Modern China*. I have reedited them all, added cross-references, and removed all the characters to various charts and tables in the back. In addition, several of these chapters were only published in truncated form; they have now been restored. Also, no characters were published with the *Modern China* pieces; all of the characters can now be found herein. All institutional affiliations listed in the table of contents reflect places of employment at the time these articles were initially published in Japan.

1

Ming-Qing Studies in Japan: 1983

Katayama Tsuyoshi, in *Shigaku zasshi*
93.5 (May 1984), 211-218.

A great many articles were published in the field of Ming and Qing history this past year, and I am exuberant to be the one responsible for this section of the review. Because there were so many pieces, however, I have reluctantly had to skip over a good many of them, and I hope you will all understand.

The volume, *Chūgoku shi zō no saikōsei: kokka to nōmin*[a] (A Reconstruction of the Image of Chinese History: The State and the Peasantry; ed. Chūgoku shi kenkyūkai [Chinese history study group]), brings together the views of the various members of the Chūgoku shi kenkyūkai. They see the development of Chinese history as based on the relationship of small-scale peasant agriculture and the despotic state. The small-scale management mode of production, together with various other modes of production, determined the nature of the state, while through these two pivots relations of production and social structure might come into conflict over time.

While the book needs to be reviewed as a whole, here I want to examine the views of one of the members of the study group, Adachi Keiji (including some of his work that has appeared in other journals). These include: (a) "Feudalism and Studies of Pre-Modern Chinese History"[a] (introduction to chapter 4 of this book); (b) "The Development of Agricultural Management in the Qing and Republican Periods"[b] (chapter 5 of this book); (c) "A Critical Investigation of Conceptions of Chinese Feudalism"[c] (*Rekishi hyōron* 400); and (d) "The Development of Landownership by Landlords in Suzhou Prefecture during the Qing"[d] (*Kumamoto daigaku bungakubu ronsō, shigaku* 9).

Of these four pieces, (b) and (d) are empirical studies, while (a) and (c) deal with theory. Let us look first at the empirical studies. Essay (b) makes use of the Fish-Scale Registers (*Yulin tuce*) and other materials on rural conditions for the villages of Suzhou Prefecture, and investigates the class distribution there based on various scales of management for the early Qing, the late Qing, and the 1930's. Adachi argues that, contrary to accepted theory, in the years from the early Qing through the Republican period the small-scale management mode of production was enjoying a flourishing period of firm, petty bourgeois activity. Putting aside the problem of the reliability of the sources for a moment, the argument remains incomplete insofar as he tries to show an increase both in scale of management and revenues and yet fails to mention the surpluses remaining on hand due to this system of management.

Adachi's article (d) again makes use of the Fish-Scale Registers and traces the changes in forms of landownership in Yuanhe County, Suzhou Prefecture. He argues, again contrary to accepted theories, that in the early Qing private landownership was still exercised by resident landowners, but that by the late Qing absentee landlordism prevailed. His argument concerning resident landowners in the early Qing, however, is rather difficult to sustain. Furthermore, although he argues that the operations of the state functioned on a high standard, to which the detailed quality of the Fish-Scale Registers attested, without a full investigation into how these Registers were compiled, this point cannot be stated unconditionally.

Of Adachi's theoretical essays, (c) is based on the detailed findings of (a) and takes a hard look at the conceptual vocabulary used. The main point of (c) is to demonstrate that, as a result of postwar Japanese views of Chinese feudalism itself, the state and society of pre-modern China cannot be conceived of as feudal. He then provides an alternative explanation. First, he suggests (and explains) two kinds of *dependence* (as opposed to control). These are public dependence and individual dependence, both indicating "personal subservience." Public dependence (or public control) refers to the "reproduction" [see fn. 8 below] of the conditions of the social existence surrounding small-scale management, such as water control and irrigation, military protection, maintenance of the system of the social division of labor, coordination of the mutual benefits of small-scale management, and the like. These depend on the public administrative, military, and civil jurisprudential controlling authority within a defined locality. With public dependence as its basic condition, small-scale management exploited surplus labor. Individual dependence was a dependency of bondservants (part-time or full-time laborers) on their masters who as small-scale managers were directly in charge of the production process. Thus, he argues that "feudalism" is conceptually concerned with public control insofar as public control is realized through each individual privately.

Following these conceptual stipulations, Adachi then critically examines Niida Noboru's thesis that the landlord-tenant system in China was feudal, Oyama Masaaki's position on the formation of feudalism in the late Ming and early Qing period, and Shigeta Atsushi's view of the establishment of feudal control by local gentry-landlords in the late Ming and early Qing. He claims they confused these two kinds of dependence, or distinguished them only vaguely or incompletely. Adachi himself denies the existence of feudalism in Chinese history.

In other words, Adachi's argument is that in Chinese society the "central portion" (*chūshin bubun*—I have certain reservations about the use of this expression) of the various tasks involved in social "reproduction" was implemented by the state through the exaction of taxes and labor service (the surplus labor) from small-scale management: "public rule" was not parcellized. Thus, "feudal society (Japan, Europe) and a society with an advanced despotic state form (China) are not two stages of development that take the autonomy of small-scale management as parameters, but they are different types of development." In place of the diagram plotting the transition from feudalism to capitalism, Adachi proposes (with several reservations) as a more general schema one that plots a course from the development of small-scale management to capitalism. He concludes that we need a distinctive elucidation of the development of small-scale management as well as empirical examinations of the various aspects of the state's "public rule" that counterbalanced it.

Over the past few years, Adachi has argued that from Ming and Qing onward small-scale agrarian management rapidly developed into a petty bourgeois system based on small commercial production. The foregoing argument attempts to reorganize and resolve the issue of control and dependence surrounding small-scale management. He has scrutinized small-scale management's development in great detail and has turned up many points worthy of study. Furthermore, I am basically in agreement with the position of those who are trying to liberate studies of pre-modern Chinese history from the shackles of [conceptions of] feudalism.

This position presumes that several things are true. Most basic among them is that from the Song dynasty on the "community" (*kyōdōtai*) in the narrow sense was broken up (Adachi sees the despotic state as *kyōdōtai* in the broad sense), and the state became more consolidated and more centralized as it controlled and organized the land and the people in a unified way (see his article [a]). He regards even the *li-chia* system as a man-made creation based on the unified control and organization of the state. Accordingly, if this part of his argument can be refuted, then Adachi's position falls apart.

We could point to several essays that have posited *kyōdōtai* relations for the Ming-Qing period, but I would like to look at my own work in this field. From an analysis of the *tujia* system of the Pearl River delta, equivalent to the *lijia* system elsewhere,[1] I have tried to show that lineage organization (as *kyōdōtai*) authoritatively intervened between the state, on the one hand, and individual families and the land on the other. While I admit that the *tujia* system of the Pearl River delta was rather exceptional, this question is most important to an understanding of the *lijia* system, and I wonder how Adachi would deal with the following problem which has been ignored to this point. The compilation of the Yellow Registers for taxes and *corveé* was carried out once every ten years. Although some ownership rights to land changed through sale within this period of time, neither the tax burden on the household that sold the land nor on the village in which the household was resident were revised when the next Yellow Register was compiled. In other words, this inconsistency in the registers in what was levied from the household or village was *systemic*. Characteristically, it ought to have been resolved apart from state institutions within the *lijia* structure or between villages. As I have already noted, the *tujia* system of the Pearl River delta suggests this conceptual model. It may be that social relations and the social structure (*kyōdōtai*) that made possible such a function there existed in other localities as well.

"The Deportation of Rich Families to Beijing in the Early Ming"[a] (*Tōyō gakuhō* 64.1-2), by Satō Manabu, analyzes the deportation of rich families to Beijing in the first year of the Yongle reign [1403], with a particular attention to the state's policies toward rich families in the early Ming.

"The World of the *Zhengshi guifan*: Ming State Power and the Rich"[a] by Danjō Hiroshi (in *Min-Shin jidai*) uses the material found in the text of the *Zhengshi guifan* to suggest concrete evidence for the concept raised by Mori Masao of *chiiki shakai* (local society or *kyōdōtai*).[2] He argues that Chinese society from the late Yuan through the mid-Ming was dominated by rich families consciously concerned with village maintenance. Because of the vertical bond between the rich (landlords) and the people, this consciousness of the social order was enforced under a *mutual* understanding of the coexistence of both sides. Among the rich families, those who possessed such a consciousness were concerned with village maintenance, and Ming state power regulated and preserved this ideal of the social order from outside the village. The social and economic conditions for this consciousness of the social order lay in the fact that rich families and landlords resided in villages. One might sum up as a temporal characteristic of the early Ming the fact that dynastic authority represented this consciousness of the social order in its highest form.

I would like to mention three points of my own in this connection. First, might not the conceptual unit of "the rich" (*fumin*) best be understood not as an individual status but as a lineage one? Second, Danjō's content analysis of the common ownership *character* of the Zhengs' land is incomplete. Might we not interpret the historical materials presented in the following way? As to actual ownership, each piece of land reverted to individual members of the lineage; however, in the event of a purchase, lineage members reported to their lineage organization and left in the care of the paterfamilias an "industrial bond." The lineage organization thereby controlled the amount of land owned by lineage members (taxes were paid by the lineage as a whole); and it prevented individual sales by lineage members in that the land was considered formally and conceptually to be the property of the entire body of lineage descendants. This may all be surmised from the fact that the brothers Zheng Qin and Zheng Zhu contributed over eight *qing* of land for the purpose of a public objective, the Jiali estate. Third, if we were to call the rich families' concern for village maintenance the disposition or intentionality of individual men, then the primary cause of it would have to be chance. (The same applies to Mori Masao's work in this vein). He ought rather to have considered in his notion of *local society* that what was more fundamentally and more generically owned in common (including the common people as well here) was the basic principle of the Zhengs' lineage itself (referred to by Danjō in his footnote 27).

"The History of a Locality"[a] (*Shakai keizai shigaku* 49.2) by Ueda Makoto takes the example of Zhongyi *hsiang*, Fenghua County, Zhejiang to set the groundwork for subsequent work elucidating the relationship between the structure of local society and lineage cohesion. He points out that because of the difference in migration times after the Tang, permanent abodes, land development, and social relations within population centers all varied. There is much worthy of study in Ueda's employment of a geographical methodology.

My essay "Various Contradictions in the Tujia System and Its Reform in the Pearl River Delta of Guangdong in the Late Qing"[c] (*Kainan shigaku* 21) relies on the case of Foshan fortress, Nanhai County, in which the *tujia* system had continued in its typical fashion over a long period of time. I examine the conspicuous appearance of men who from the mid-Qing on became free from the control of the *tujia* system (or lineage organization) by founding *linghu* or "additional households." I also look at the response of the *tujia* system to this phenomenon. In 1982 Kobayashi Yoshihiro made opportune and important suggestions in the field of Song history regarding problems of research on lineage. In my own view we must not think of all lineages as largely the same in character and fundamental principles; nor can we merely refer to the birth of the gentry class (*xiangshen* or *shenshi*) as the result of chance. We must examine the substantive nature of individual lineage organizations, looking into such issues as variation based on times of migration.

The following three essays appeared in the volume *Zoku Chūgoku minshū hanran no sekai* (The World of Popular Rebellion in China, Continued),[a] edited by the Seinen Chūgoku kenkyūsha kaigi (Conference of Young China Scholars): Sōda Hiroshi, "The Formation and Development of the Luo Sect"[a]; Satō Kimihiko, "The Historical Development of the White Lotus Sect in the Qing Dynasty: The Eight Trigrams Sect and Various Uprisings"[a]; and Kobayashi Kazumi, "The Rebellion of Qi Wangshi: An Introduction to Research on the White Lotus Rebellion of the Jiaqing Era"[a].

Sōda examines the doctrines of the Luo Sect which exerted a major influence on popular religion in the latter half of the Ming dynasty. He raises two points as especially characteristic of Luo doctrine: (1) a belief in ontological "emptiness" (*kong*) and a notion that all things belonged to the same unity—these ideas relativized phenomena, removed distinct boundaries of reality, and denied (indeed, destroyed) established order and value; and (2) an enlightenment based on the workings of each individual's "mind" (*xin*)—a stress on the autonomy of the individual. Regarding these two points Sōda notes that there is a resemblance both to the idea of a "benevolence of all things belonging to a single unity" of the Wang Yang-ming school (an established ideology at that time) as well as to the trend in the "New Buddhism" toward seeing the unity of the three teachings. He also argues that the formation of these doctrines was influenced by the development of a monetary economy from the mid-Ming on, since a monetary economy simultaneously quantified and relativized all things, while it brought about the development of the autonomous consciousness of each individual. This latter point echoes one raised some time ago by Ono Kazuko concerning the influence exerted by a monetary economy on the Wang Yangming school.

Satō's article provides indispensable groundwork for future research into popular religious associations of the Qing dynasty by clarifying as much as presently possible the temporal and spatial development of the spread of religious networks. Satō examines the Eight Trigrams Sect, the largest White Lotus school in North China during the Qing. As for the various religious associations which hitherto could only be vaguely referred to as "branches of the White Lotus," it has now become possible on the basis of this work to understand in rather concrete terms the individual historical quality of these religious networks as well as the mutual relations between them. We hope to see further work in this area in the future.

Kobayashi's essay traces the career of Qi Wangshi, a woman and leading religious teacher of the Xiangyang religious army of Hubei Province. He goes on to point out that the White Lotus Rebellion of the Jiaqing period was not a rebellion endowed with a generally positive outlook—based on values of independence, rationality, action, spontaneity, and the like. In fact, the rebels looked with regret on what had been lost, a concave magnetic field (not a convex course of direction). Theirs was a deeply humanistic spirit, a mode of thought that regarded as irrelevent any concern for progress or development. Furthermore, he proposes that the movement for the recovery of human nature at a single stroke is in keeping with the ahistorical quality possessed by the floating social strata of street performers, yamen underlings, scribes, and inhabitants of the underworld. Yet, the historical quality of the direct producers gives a historical phase to their movement.

Yoshio Hiroshi's essay "Notes on Research on Roving Bandits in the Late Ming"[a] (*Kōnan joshi tanki daigaku kiyō* 12) is based on research into the Liuliu Liuqi Rebellion of the mid-Ming and the Nian Rebellion of the late Qing. In order to explain the basis for the rise of banditry in the late Ming and to understand society in North China at that time, Yoshio focuses attention again on *youmin* (also referred to as *wulai* and *guanggun*), a non-agricultural group of people who formed one part of the basis of local bandits' power. He notes the need for investigations of their particular qualities in the late Ming.

Satō Fumitoshi looks into the structural characteristics of the rebellious Changpanzi and its dissolution and reorganization in the process of the establishment of Li Zicheng's regime, in his essay "Peasant Rebellion in the Late Ming and Changpanzi"[a] (in *Sakuma*). His attention to questions of organization is extremely interesting.

In his essay "A Look at Village Temples in China"[a] (*Kindai Chūgoku kenkyū ihō* 5), Hamashima Atsutoshi clears up several points concerning the belief in *zongguan*[3] which he takes to have been widespread in Jiangnan villages during the Ming and Qing eras. This belief originated in the late Yuan and early Ming through the extraordinary capacity of the "governors" to protect shipments of the land tax monies. In general, this belief took form where the control over villages and the peasantry was exercised by the local resident landlord stratum (*liangzhang*[4]); it changed as resident landlord authority dissolved in the late Ming and early Qing; this eventually resulted in a concentration of tenant farmers involved in anti-rent struggles in the late Qing. We hope that in further studies Hamashima will look at how the religious beliefs surrounding the *zongguan* underwent change as the believers became tenant farmers.

He has also written an essay entitled "A Brief Introduction to the *Puyang yandu* [Court archives at Puyang], Held in the Beijing Library: On Tenancy Relations"[b] (*Hokkaidō daigaku bungakubu kiyō* 32.1). This essay introduces and examines some important historical material.

Okuzaki Yūji has written an essay entitled "Standards for Money-Making in the Late Ming and Early Qing: One Aspect of the Ledgers of Merit and Demerit"[a] (in *Sakuma*). After demonstrating the subtle shifts from late Ming to early Qing in the content of the standards within the Ledgers of Merit and Demerit, Okuzaki explores changes in gentry consciousness at this time and corresponding changes in society.

In his essay "The Emergence of Benevolent Societies (*shanhui*) and Benevolent Halls (*shantang*)"[a] (in *Min-Shin jidai*), Fuma Susumu points out that the Fangsheng hui (societies for releasing life), Yan'ge hui (burial societies), Iming futu hui, Jiushengchuan (boats for saving drowning people), Xuli hui (societies for the care of widows), Puji tang (poor houses), and Yuying tang (foundling homes) were all *shanhui* or *shantang* with the same relief systems as the Tongshan hui and with a structure aimed at doing "good deeds." He also makes the point that the late Ming and early Qing when *shanhui* and *shantang* grew up in many places was a time when men tried to cope with the problems of a single locality by means of local gentry assemblies (*gongyi*). Fuma keenly notes that because this structure of "good deeds" was "a realm conceived of as differences in point credits," there was the danger that it could lead to activity based solely on the desire to increase one's points. As we saw in the essay by Sōda Hiroshi above, among the major tasks for future research will be to see the origins of problems concerning quantification and relativization in the late Ming and early Qing and to see the extent to which they permeated and influenced various aspects of society.

Mizoguchi Yūzō's essay, "Conceptions of Human Nature in the Ming and Qing Periods"[a] (in *Sakuma*), deals with the views of human nature held by representative intellectuals in the Ming and Qing. He explores two trends: toward a stress on cultivated behavior and toward an affirmation of social ambition (wealth, honor, and so on). He points out that the themes concerning human nature (introduced in the Song dynasty) reached fruition around the time of Dai Zhen, and made possible an avenue for the discussion in subsequent generations of issues concerning politics, economy, and society.

We have two essays by Ōtani Toshio: "Idealism and Realism among the Qing Local Gentry"[a] (in *Chūgoku shitaifu*); and "A Study of Scholarship in Yangzhou and Changzhou and Its Links to Society"[b] (in *Min-Shin jidai*). The first essay examines three debates—on feudalism, on the well-field system, and on cliques and parties—which were pursued by local gentry in the late Ming and early Qing, and which by the late Qing had developed, respectively, into issues of local autonomy, common ownership of land, and the activities of study associations. What position Ōtani assigns the "local" gentry within the general body of *xiangshen* and *shenshi* remains a problem in the field of intellectual history too. His second essay makes several points concerning Yangzhou and Changzhou scholarship during the Qing dynasty. Their basic characteristic was comprehensiveness in learning. While inheriting views from the late Ming and early Qing that affirmed personal ambition, they called for a reconstruction of the moral-ethical order through a re-evaluation of the *Xunzi*. This served as a vehicle for the late Qing statecraft school. Finally, he notes their social involvement with the lively commercial activities of Huizhou merchants in Yangzhou and Changzhou.

Ono Kazuko has also written two essays: "The Donglin Clique and Zhang Juzheng"[a] (in *Min-Shin jidai*); and "On the Donglin Clique (2): The Process of Its Formation"[b] (*Tōhō gakuhō* 55). Her first essay examines the search for a new political system at the end of the Ming by looking at the differences between Zhang Juzheng and the Donglin clique over the issue of Zhang's implementation of the method for evaluating officials' performances (*kaocheng fa*).[5] She notes that while Zhang sought a state with a strong centralized authority in which power was concentrated in the Grand Secretariat, the Donglin people gave priority to the interests of the locality and the populace (or *tianxia* in their usage), with power flowing from the locality to the center (the power of the sovereign). As a method for realizing and guaranteeing this, the Donglin clique sought to open and expand *yanlu* (the pipeline for political criticism). In her second article, Ono argues that after the death of Zhang Juzheng his *kaocheng fa* was abandoned and the repression of political criticism continued. As a result the Donglin clique moved from calling for open *yanlu* toward the consolidation of a Donglin "party" that moved from political criticism to power politics.

The Korean scholar Kim Jong-bak has written an essay (translated by Yamane Yukio and Inada Hideko) entitled "The Donglin Party Rivalry and Its Social Background in the Ming (1)"[a] (*Mindai shi kenkyū* 11) which examines the Donglin party with particular concern for the development of commerce and industry.

Taniguchi Kikuo has written two essays: "Lü Kun's Cadastral Survey and Rural Reform"[a] (in *Min-Shin jidai*); and "On the Xiangjia System of Lü Kun"[b] (in *Sakuma*). Both essays examine the various reform plans, in the face of North China's rural crisis, that were put forward by Lü Kun. Taniguchi sees Lü as a unique thinker in the Wanli reign period and as a member of the Donglin clique. His analysis combines investigation of Donglin thought with analysis of rural reform in the late Ming. Further research from this perspective can be expected in the future.

Ishibashi Takao's article, "On the Formative Period of the Eight *gūsa* and the Eight *gūsa* Colors"[a] (*Chūgoku kindai shi kenkyū* 3), examines the formation of the eight *gūsa* (or eight-banner) system and its color distinctions, which generally is dated prior to the first year of the Tianming reign (1616). On the basis of an investigation of historical materials (some destroyed and some touched up), he argues that this system was formed in the year 1618 and that it was an aspect of a decision to consolidate a military organization to attack the Ming. He also argues that the eight-banner color scheme was arrived at in the year 1622 and that it spelled the consolidation of the eight-banner system not only as a military organization but also as a political and social one for control over Han Chinese agricultural society on the Liaodong plain.

In his essay "The Center and the Locality in the Qing Financial Administration: The System of Equitable Allocations"[a] (*Tōyō shi kenkyū* 42.2), Iwai Shigeki makes several points: by virtue of the regulations for "equitable allocation" (*zhuobo*) of 1724, a system of seasonal report registers was instituted; because of this, centralized control by the Bureau of Finance emerged in the state financial administration; and this situation essentially continued until just prior to the Taiping Rebellion.

We also have a very interesting essay by Namiki Yorihisa: "On Tribute Grain in Henan in the Qing Dynasty"[a] (*Tōyō daigaku Tōyō shi kenkyū hōkoku* II). He presumes that the method of levying grain tribute from the peasantry in the various departments and counties of Henan Province diverged from its original principle and over time was converted to silver payment instead of grain. He argues that this was contrary to the original purpose of collecting a grain tribute. Instead it gradually became the framework for preserving improperly elevated levels of tax collection in silver in the departments and counties as well as insuring provincial military and civil funds in the late Qing period. He examines the phenomenon of the decentralization of power from the center within each province beginning in the mid-Qing, with the key being the contradiction born of the conversion to payment in silver.

Hoshi Ayao's essay, "The Development of Relief Granaries in the Early Qing: The Reserve Granaries (*yubei cang*) and the Ever Normal Granaries (*changping cang*)"[b] (*Tōyō daigaku daigakuin kiyō* 19), clarifies two points by means of an investigation of local gazetteers and historical records: (1) the role played by the reserve granaries in the early Qing was a rather large one; and (2) the creation and spread of ever normal granaries were supported by the state purchase of grain on the market (*caimai*)[6] as well as by monies derived from *jiansheng* who from the Yongzheng reign on received their status by paying the government an impost (*juanjian*).[7] By the Qianlong reign period, these types of granaries had become in name and reality the core of relief programs.

In his essay "An Introduction to Studies of the Community Granary System of the Qing Dynasty"[a] (*Mindai shi kenkyū* 11), Iemuro Shigeo first outlines the scope of the community granary system and its operational procedures. He then demonstrates that the Qing court's intent in implementing the community granary system was to guarantee the peasantry's "reproductive capacity"[8] by protecting the wealthy households of landlords and rich merchants in times of famine, so preserving the social order.

Mori Masao's essay, "Mid-Ming Reforms in the System of Land Tax Collection in Jiangnan"[a] (in *Min-Shin jidai*), traces in substantive terms the changes in land tax collection in the two prefectures of Suzhou and Songjiang from the middle of the 15th century through the middle of the 16th. He points out that behind the reforms in these systems was the contradiction of an unequal tax burden wherein a light burden was concentrated in the large households on private lands and a heavy burden was assessed small households on public land. He defines the small household stratum as including unprivileged landlords, self-cultivator owners, or tenant farmers in local society, while the large household stratum tended to be socially privileged landholders whose incomes derived from tenants, and who were moving from residence in rural villages to residence in cities. Mori's work fills in three blanks spots in previous research in this area, and we hope that his future work will clarify the nature of the social privilege enjoyed by the large household stratum (e.g., was it hereditary?), and look into the causes for change in their forms of residence.

Kuroki Kuniyasu's essay, "The Historical Significance of the Establishment of a System Whereby the State Employed Laborers with Funds Derived from Those Buying Their Way out of *Corveé* in 16th Century China"[a] (*Shigaku kenshū* 94), estimates that because of the establishment of self-sufficient, small-scale peasant management in the late Ming, the majority of the employed labor force derived from this were no longer bonded public servants but became indentured servants able to acquire wages. This historical background made possible payment in silver for the government's labor service, namely the Single Whip System.

Nishimura Kazuyo's article, "On Bondservants in the Late Ming and Early Qing"[a] (in *Min-Shin jidai*), examines the types of bondservants (*nupu*) and their systematic regulation in the Qing dynasty after the bondservant uprisings (*nubian*). She also investigates the significance of the bondservant rebellions in the late Ming and early Qing.

Terada Hiroaki has written a painstaking study entitled "The Legal Character of Topsoil and Subsoil Practices: A Conceptual Analysis"[a] (*Tōyō bunka kenkyūjo kiyō* 93). He attempts to place the one-field two-owners system of landholding conceptually within the logic of old China's overall practices concerning land law. His historical technique is marvelous and his main points may be summed up as follows. First, the on-going debate between Kusano Yasushi and Fujii Hiroshi over the one-field two-owners system is trying to establish the basis of authority of the tenant who held topsoil rights, and Terada himself agrees with this direction. Second, the expressions *ye* and *guanye* were concepts pointing to both the object and the source of revenues based on a specific system of revenue collection, but were not necessarily connected to the land itself. Thus, in the buying and selling of various rights customary at that time, purchase transferring *ye* was more common than that accomplishing transfers in the land itself. Third, topsoil and subsoil in their structure corresponded to the structure of *guanye* in that they were appropriate respectively to management earnings from tenant cultivation on the land and to earnings from the management of tenant rents. Tenant cultivation, unrelated to control over topsoil, was conducted in this sense with the legitimacy of a property right, and it was passed from tenant to tenant through sale. Fourth, legitimacy in topsoil property rights, he concludes, corresponded to a situation wherein tenant cultivation became a self-regulating management among various forms of tenant cultivation and rent relations of that time; and it might be placed at one pole among the various legal property rights either given by landowners or obtained by tenants. Two parts of Fujii Hiroshi's continuing essay, "The Basic Structure of the One-Field Two-Owners System (8, 9)"[a] (*Kindai Chūgoku* 13, 14), also deal with this issue.

In his essay "A Study of Taiwan in the Mid-Qing Period"[a] (*Tōyō gakuhō* 64.3-4), Kurihara Jun, overcoming the limitations of source materials, examines the formation of the one-field two-owners system in the Zhanghua region of Taiwan during the Daoguang reign, with a particular focus on the evolution of tenant households into small renting households.

Finally, let me add that we need full-fledged book reviews of two volumes: *Sakuma* (in which a number of essays are concerned with the history of ceramics) and *Min-Shin jidai*, both cited above.

2

Japanese Studies of Post-Opium War China: 1983

Harigaya Miwako, in *Shigaku zasshi*
93.5 (May 1984), 218-24.

Over the past few years we have reflected upon the appropriate methodology for understanding the "modern period" in China. Two essays among a number in 1983 were concerned with this issue: Mizoguchi Yūzō, "Isn't Our Image of Modern China Distorted?: Early Westernization (*yangwu*) and People's Rights, 'Chinese Learning as the Basis, Western Learning as the Instrument' (*Zhong-ti Xiyong*) and Confucianism"[b] (*Rekishi to shakai* 2); and Hamashita Takeshi, "Modern Asian Markets and England"[a] (*Shikai* 30).

Mizoguchi argues that because the "search for the origins of Mao's revolution" has occupied central stage in postwar studies of modern China, especially in intellectual history, our image of modern China has been distorted. The late Qing revolutionary movement has been detached and made into a "monistic historical conception of popular revolution" and the "historical era of the Qing" has been fully misunderstood. The "reform and self-strengthening" efforts of men like Li Hongzhang and Zhang Zhidong have been thoroughly denigrated. Mizoguchi points out the problems in a "historical evaluation" that simply dismisses such men as the leaders of the Westernization group (*yangwu pai*) and the supporters of the Qing's "anti-popular regime." He notes that it is a pressing task of modern Chinese historical studies to "construct an overarching perspective" of the three hundred year-long process of Qing history. He also considers the methodological task of generating a overall view of the internal development of Chinese history from the pre-modern to the modern era.

Hamashita, on the other hand, reflects methodologically on our understanding of external causes at work in Asia in the modern period, ordinarily said to have begun with the "Western impact." He points out that it is insufficient to set that "impact" against the internal development of the various Asian countries; rather, by grasping Asian history as "a historical entity held together by a single organic bond," he sees the West responding to an "Asian impact," shining light on the West from the perspective of Asia.

Using economic history, in particular market issues, he demonstrates that there was a single national historical modernity in Asia: a modern Asian market based on the Western entrance into the pre-modern Asian market, the reorganization of the pre-modern market, and its incorporation into world markets. Given this mutual interpenetration of the modern Western world and Asia, understood on an Asia-wide scale, he notes that we should now deepen our knowledge of the relationship between the pre-modern and modern eras as it affected national issues as well as global ones.

Like Mizoguchi, who argues that we need to see the modern period in China as structurally inseparable from a distinctive pre-modern period, and that both are qualitatively different from those of Europe, Hamashita is also looking for a basic perspective for comprehending the modern history of China. Our effort to come to an understanding of the totality of the modern era in China will, I think, necessitate bringing together the arguments of both men and presenting concrete evidence to bear on their positions. Let me now proceed to examine research, primarily from 1983, in the various disciplines.

First, in the field of economic history, let us take a look at articles dealing with land systems and agricultural management. Terada Hiroaki's essay, "The Legal Character of Topsoil and Subsoil Practices: A Conceptual Analysis"[a] (*Tōyō bunka kenkyūjo kiyō* 93), is a painstaking study of topsoil and subsoil practices in the land systems from the late Ming through the early Republic. He places this one-field two-owners system within the overall body of contemporaneous legal practice. He also offers a resolution of the debate between Fujii Hiroshi and Kusano Yasushi by discussing the concepts of topsoil and non-topsoil and the origins of the legitimacy of tenant cultivation.[1]

In his essay, "Various Contradictions in the Tujia System and Its Reform in the Pearl River Delta of Guangdong in the Qing (Nanhai County)"[c] (*Kainan shigaku* 21), Katayama Tsuyoshi analyzes the problems of the *tujia* system (comparable to the *lijia* system elsewhere) from the mid-Qing on. He argues that the system was maintained by members of lineage organizations in the Pearl River delta.

Enatsu Yoshiki has also written an article in this field: "The Social and Economic Significance of the Disposal of Public Lands in the Southern Portion of the Three Northeastern Provinces in the Late Qing: The Case of the Jinzhou Manor"[a] (*Shakai keizai shigaku* 49.4). He investigates the disposal through sale (*zhangfang*) to the public of one official manor that comprised an important financial base for the Qing dynasty. He shows that the local authorities in Manchuria built an economic foundation for the Guangxu Emperor's regime while reorganizing the resident landlord stratum (the "managers" of the former manor).

Namiki Yorihisa's essay, "On Tribute Grain in Henan in the Qing

Dynasty"[a] (*Tōyō daigaku Tōyōshi kenkyū hōkoku* II), elucidates changes in the system by which tribute grain was collected in Henan as well as the realities of collection.

Important works discussing the local gentry in the late Qing would include Shinmura Ireko, "The Historical Nature of the *Jushi* in Late Qing Sichuan"[a] (*Tōyō gakuhō* 64.3-4). She explains who the *jushi* were: one to three men were selected from the gentry for every bureau (*ju*) and with the support of the local officialdom they carried out, through the bureau, a host of local administrative functions including tax collection, public welfare, education, and the maintenance of public security. She argues that after the White Lotus Rebellion and the peasant rebellions of the 1850's, the *jushi* reorganized the landlord system and once again consolidated their control over the local village.

Next, let us look at articles dealing with industrialization in the late Qing. In her essay, "The Activities of British Capital in China in the 1860's: The Management of the Jardine-Matheson Silk Mill"[a] (*Ochanomizu shigaku* 26-27), Ishii Mayako uses letters of the Jardine-Matheson Company to clarify the activities of the company silk mill in Shanghai from 1859 to 1869. She discusses such issues as business conditions, the personal background and temperament of Mr. John Major who managed the mill, the hiring of laborers, and the purchase of raw cocoons. She concludes that the mill failed because such things as transactions over cocoons and raw silk thread were impeded by the guild regulations of privileged merchants.

Nagai Nobuhiro's article, "The Official-Supervising Merchant-Management (*guandu shangban*) System of the Era of Early Westernization: The Bureau of the Kaiping Mines in Zhili"[a] (*Rekishi kagaku to kyōiku* 2), analyzes the management of the Kaiping Mines Bureau, established in 1879. He argues that the historical significance of the *guandu shangban* system lay in its enabling within China's dynastic system the development of national capital through the solicitation of capital from the public.

As regards studies of the establishment of railways, we have Nomura Tōru's "A Study of the Song-Hu Railway"[a] (in *Sakuma*). One skillful essay examining past Japanese research in economic history is Yoshida Kōichi, "Trends in Japanese Research into the Economic History of Modern and Contemporary China (1): Agriculture"[a] (*Atarashii rekishigaku no tame ni* 170).

Let us now examine studies in the field of political history. Sasaki Masaya's continuing essay, "A Study of the Opium War: From the Arrival of Pottinger to the Signing of the Treaty of Nanjing (Part 1)"[a] (*Kindai Chūgoku* 14), treats events from the perspectives of both the Chinese and the English governments. It covers the period from the dismissal of British

Plenipotentiary Elliot and the removal and arrest of Imperial Commissioner Qishan for having overstepped his bounds through the arrival of Pottinger. In his article, "The Alliance Policy Advocated by Chinese Reformers in the Late 19th Century"[a] (*Tōyō shi kenkyū* 42.1), Pak Jong-hyûn follows the process by which Kang Youwei, Liang Qichao, and the late Qing reformers attempted to use the influence of the Powers and effect reforms in China. He examines the changes in their positions on foreign alliances.

Fujioka Kikuo, in his essay "Zhang Jian and the Southeast Guarantee"[a] (in *Sakuma*), examines the facts behind Zhang Jian's persuasion of Liang-Jiang Governor-General Liu Kun'i to sign the "Southeast Guarantee."

Hatano Yoshihiro, in "Wang Zhaoming [Jingwei] during the Period of the 1911 Revolution"[a] (*Aichi gakuin daigaku bungakubu kiyō* 12), diligently explores Wang's activities and his underlying understanding of events. With the outbreak of the Wuchang Uprising, Wang attempted to use Yuan Shikai to establish a republic. He played a pivotal role in the North-South negotiations leading to the establishment of a unified North-South republican government.

Two other articles look at the 1911 era from different angles. First, there is Matsumoto Takehiko's "The 1911 Revolution and the Overseas Chinese in Kōbe around the Time of the Wuchang Uprising"[a] (*Chūgoku kenkyū geppō* 425). He clarifies the contribution to the revolution of the overseas Chinese by examining the activities of the Unified Alliance of Overseas Chinese Merchants and the facts surrounding the dispatch of the Dare-to-Die Corps. Second, Kojima Yoshio traces the activities of the Chinese National Assembly in Shanghai, in his essay "On the Chinese National Assembly (Part 2)"[a] (*Shingai kakumei kenkyū* 3).

There are two new guides to research on the 1911 Revolution: Ichiko Chūzō, "New Chinese Publications on the 1911 Revolution"[a] (*Kindai Chūgoku kenkyū ihō* 5); and Yamane Yukio, ed., *Shimpen Shingai kakumei bunken mokuroku* (A Bibliography of Materials on the 1911 Revolution).[a]

One essay which is concerned with the period from the 1911 Revolution through the May Fourth Movement is Ajioka Tōru's "The Collapse of the Financial Administration of Yuan Shikai's Government and the Order to Suspend Specie Payment"[a] (in *Masubuchi*). He argues that Yuan Shikai's order to suspend specie payment of both the Bank of China and the Communications Bank was issued with the objective of breaking out of the fierce monetary straitjacket caused by Yuan's imperial movement and the war of "national protection." The suspension gave rise to fiscal chaos and accelerated the collapse of Yuan's regime as well as the decline of the faction around Liang Shiyi.

Another essay by Ajioka, entitled "The Revival of Local Autonomy After the War of National Protection: Jiangsu Province"[b] (*Chūō daigaku jimbun kenkyū kiyō* 2), deals with a related issue. He argues that in the aftermath of the war of national protection, the movement for the revival of the institutions of local autonomy, such as provincial assemblies led by the local gentry, constituted a struggle for the protection of "democracy" against warlord authority.

Two articles dealing with the period of the May Fourth Movement which appeared in *Chūō daigaku jimbun kenkyū kiyō* (2), are: Nozawa Yutaka, "The May Fourth Movement and Provincial Assemblies: Toward an Investigation of the Inner Structure of the National Movement"[a]; and Kasahara Tokushi, "The Movement Opposing Sino-Japanese Military Cooperation: The Unfolding of the Chinese National Movement on the Eve of the May Fourth Movement."[a] Nozawa examines the role played by the provincial assemblies in the May Fourth period by looking at the relationship between the anti-Japanese national movement and the popular movement. He sees the national revolution from the perspective of the May Fourth Movement. Kasahara stresses the importance of the opposition to Sino-Japanese military cooperation in the May Fourth period, and he sees this movement from the perspectives of the activities of the National Salvation Group of Chinese students in Japan as well as the splintered resistance to warlord power.

Two further essays examine political and economic policies in the May Fourth period with an eye to the influence of the Russian Revolution in China. They are Kasahara Tokushi, "Sino-Japanese Military Cooperation and the Beijing Government's 'Retraction of Self-Government in Outer Mongolia': One Perspective on the Changes in the World of East Asia Engendered by the Russian Revolution"[b] (*Rekishigaku kenkyū* 515); and Ajioka Tōru, "The 'Recovery of the Right to Print Money' in the Northern Part of the Three Northeastern Provinces after the Russian Revolution"[c] (*Rekishigaku kenkyū* 513).

In the field of intellectual history, quite a number of essays examine the late Qing period. Among those concerned with Zhang Binglin is Ebitani Naonori, "The Formation of Zhang Binglin's Racialism, from 1898 through the *Subao* Case"[a] (*Tōyō bunka* N. S. 51). He traces Chang's early revolutionary thought from his break with the movement for reform within the system to his advocacy of an anti-Manchu racialist revolution.

Satō Yutaka has written "Zhang Binglin, Notes on the Theory of Evolution"[a] (*Byōtōō* 2). Satō examines the development of Zhang's thought, centering on the issue of evolutionary theory, and he argues that Zhang rejected evolutionism by focusing on the "nature of what was proper" (*dangweixing*).

One further examination of Zhang Binglin is: Harashima Haruo, "Scholarship and Revolution in Zhang Taiyan: From 'Sorrow' (*ai*) to 'Loneliness' (*jimo*)"[a] (*Shisō* 708). According to Harashima, while Zhang advocated an anti-Manchu revolution based on the principle of "history as the autonomous realm of the ethnic group" (*minzu*), he also aimed at a bourgeois revolution to overthrow the feudal system. Faced with the realities of imperialist invasion, Zhang felt pressured to "overstep the bourgeois revolution" and eventually he moved "to relativize" the state, nationalism, and revolution, using "the logic of consciousness-only Buddhism and the world of negation." In so doing, Harashima argues, Zhang denied all values associated with modernity.

Harashima has also written on the relationship of modern society and Lin Zexu in his piece, "A Short Study of Lin Zexu"[b] (*Rōhyakusei no sekai* 1). Here, he locates in Lin's thought a guarantee for the "advantage" of the "populace" through the rational use of the "powers" of "officials."

We also have an essay by Abe Ken'ichi that examines Zou Rong, the man implicated with Zhang Binglin in the *Subao* case: "Zou Rong's *The Revolutionary Army* and Modern Western Thought: *The Social Contract* and the Theory of Evolution"[a] (*Seiji keizai shigaku* 200). Abe argues that *The Revolutionary Army*, relying on *The Social Contract* of Rousseau and the *Tianyan lun* (On Evolution) of Yan Fu, called for anti-Manchu racial revolution based on the return of the natural rights of mankind. It advocated the simultaneous realization of a Han ethnic state and a republican form of government.

Kusunose Masaaki has written on a contemporary of Zou Rong in his article, "The Sufferings of an Intellectual in the Early Republican Period: A Look at Huang Yuanyong"[a] (*Ajia kenkyū* 3). He argues that Huang called for the "destruction of political parties" out of disillusionment with the established parties, which were unable to transform politics under Yuan Shikai after the 1911 Revolution. Eventually, though, Huang understood that the responsibility for the "darkness" of actual politics in his day belonged to the nation itself. This opened the way for him to see a transformation and progression in the national consciousness through the personal transformation of intellectuals having undergone "penitence."

We have two pieces on Tan Sitong: Sakamoto Hiroko, "One Aspect of Modern Chinese Thought: Tan Sitong's Conception of *yitai* (Ether)"[a] (*Shisō* 706); and Tomita Noboru, "Tan Sitong's View of Mankind: A Look at His Notion of Breaking Through All Bonds"[a] (in *Ningensei*). Sakamoto's essay reexamines the logical structure of Tan's conception of ether; she locates the immediate origins of his idea of ether in a volume by Henry Wood, translated into Chinese by John Fryer as *Zhixin mianbing fa* (Methods to Regulate the Mind and Prevent Disorder). She goes on to illuminate the relationship, hitherto completely unmentioned, of the idea of ether to the Buddhist learning of Yang Wenhui. In an effort to understand the development of his thought, Tomita centers his analysis on Tan's notion of breaking through all bonds. He discusses the structure of Tan's thought around the "major theme of how to link" societal transformation with individual transformation; and he traces Tan's rapid development from the formation of the Nanxuehui (Southern Study Society), to his critique of Confucian morality and anti-Manchuism, his participation in the planning for a restoration, and his death.

Two articles concern Zhang Zhidong: Kotō Tomoko, "Zhang Zhidong's View of *Zhongti Xiyong*: The 'Ethics' of an Intellectual's Study of 'Western Learning'"[a] (*Komazawa daigaku gaikokugo kenkyū ronshū* 18); and Satō Ken'ichi, "Views of 'People's Rights' in the 1890's: The 'Debate' Between Zhang Zhidong and He Kai (Qi)"[a] (in *Ningensei*). Kotō argues that, for Zhang, *ti* and *yong* meant, respectively, ethics and skill, morality and technique. *Zhongxue* (Chinese learning), which Zhang associated with *ti*, included the personal ethics necessary to govern the mind and body, political ethics for governing the realm, and nativist ethics aimed at national independence, national unity, and wealth and power. Facing the critical "dismemberment" of China in the aftermath of the Sino-Japanese War, Chang looked for a route to Chinese independence and self-strengthening in the "modern bureaucratic state," led by a technical bureaucracy equipped with both the techniques of Western learning and the ethics of Chinese learning.

Satō examines the debate between Zhang Zhidong and He Kai over "people's rights" as advocated by Zheng Guanying among others. While Zhang rejected a "people's rights" that conflicted with the three bonds of traditional Chinese ethics, He affirmed "people's rights" as heaven-bestowed or "natural" rights and advocated the "right to individual autonomy" as its fulcrum. Satō concludes that these positions on "people's rights" failed to gain influence because of the "onslaught of evolutionary theory."

Harada Masaoto's article, "Japan, Southeast Asia, and Kang Youwei"[a] (*Waseda daigaku daigakuin bungaku kenkyūka kiyō* 28), discusses changes in Kang's thought as they relate to his refugee life in Japan, Singapore, Penang, and elsewhere. Harada has also written a book on Kang entitled *Kō Yūi no shisō undō to minshū* (Kang Youwei's Intellectual Movement and the Populace).[b] This volume has been reviewed by Maruyama Matsuyuki in *Chūgoku kenkyū geppō* (427).

Finally, Saitō Michihiko offers a synopsis of the existing research and source materials on Li Dazhao, in his essay "Notes on the History of Research on Li Dazhao, China Section"[a] (*Chūō daigaku jimbun kenkyū kiyō* 2).

Numerous articles concerning educational history appeared in 1983. In his essay "Clan Schools on the Eve of the Installation of the New Educational System in China" (*Kyōikugaku ronshū* 25), Taga Akigorō makes use of the "Regulations of the Charitable Estate" of the Huang family of Shanhua County, Hunan, to clarify the structure and function of traditional clan and family schools that provided the "foundations for the new educational system."

Sakaide Yoshinobu's article, "Science Education in the Late Qing: The Case of the Gezhi Academy in Shanghai"[a] (*Kansai daigaku bungaku ronshū* 32.3), describes how in the midst of the early Westernization movement new-style schools were established in various localities and adopted a modern scientific educational curriculum. Among them was the popular scientific professional school, the Gezhi Academy, founded by Xu Shou and the missionary John Fryer in Shanghai in 1875. As the principal achievements left by the Gezhi Academy, Sakaide cites its systematic science education curriculum, a collection of prize essays by Wang Tao, and the publication of *Gezhi huipian*, the first professional journal in the natural sciences in China. He also points to the influence exercised by the latter on Kang Youwei and Tan Sitong.

Sakaide has also published a volume entitled *Chūgoku kindai no shisō to kagaku* (Modern Thought and Science in China).[b] This work facilitates our understanding of the intellectual workings of Chinese thinkers in the process of accepting modern Western science from the late Qing through the early Republic, but to do justice to this book would require a separate review.

Another piece in this area is Yoshida Tora's "On the *Da Deguo xuexiao lunlue* (An Examination of the German Schools) of Missionary [Ernst] Faber in China"[a] (in *Taga*). Yoshida discusses the work of this foreign missionary who promoted the reform of educational institutions in the era of early Westernization.

Also in *Taga* we find an essay by Abe Hiroshi entitled "Education in Late Qing Schools and Instruction by Japanese Teachers: The Case of Zhili."[a] Abe discusses the activities of Japanese educators invited to China to make up for the teacher shortage in the Guangxu era.

Zeng Dexiang, in his essay "A Study of the Romanization Movement in the Late Qing"[a] (*Chūō gakuin daigaku ronsō* 18.1), describes the "movement to phoneticize the Chinese language" led by such intellectuals as Lu Zhuangzhang, who believed that China's national weakness at that time was due to the difficulty of the Chinese written language.

In "Beijing University and the Warlords: Cai Yuanpei's Reforms and the Struggle Surrounding Them"[a] (*Shirin* 32), Kobayashi Yoshifumi sheds light on the modernizing reforms undertaken by Cai Yuanpei at Beijing University and the resistance to the interference and pressure from warlord influence.

In the field of women's history, let me first point out an essay by Fukazawa Hideo, "The 1898 Reform Movement and the Chinese Women's Academy"[a] (*Arutesu riberaresu*) 32). He examines the Chinese Women's Academy, an educational organ for women, which was established with the aim of educating "good wives and wise mothers" and training talented young women.

Ishii Yōko's article, "Women Students Studying in Japan in the Period of the 1911 Revolution"[a] (*Shiron* 36), describes the activities of Chinese women students in Japan. She considers their reception there, the conditions they faced, their educational curriculum, and the magazines they published, as well as their formation of an organization aimed at "unity in the female world." In so doing, Ishii traces the process of their becoming aware of the "independence of women themselves." She also examines the influence these women exercised on the women's movement once they had returned to China.

Concerning the domestic women's liberation movement, we have a piece by Suetsugu Reiko, "A Depiction of the Women's Movement in the May Fourth Period (Part 1)"[a] (*Rekishi hyōron* 395). In this as yet unfinished essay, Suetsugu describes the growth of the women's liberation movement in its relation to the mass and national movements of the May Fourth period. She traces the development of a democratic approach to women's liberation by looking at such things as the strikes of female laborers in the Shanghai tobacco factories and textile mills, the critique of the family system as it appeared in such publications of the period as *Furen zazhi* (Women's Miscellany) and *Xinqingnian* (New Youth), and the demands for coeducation and for the franchise.

Suetsugu has also written "The Chinese Women's Movement in the May Fourth Period and Knowledge of the Russian Revolution"[b] (*Rekishigaku kenkyū* 513). In this essay she analyzes the formation of a socialist women's liberation movement in the May Fourth era which "greatly changed both the subjective and the objective conditions for the women's liberation movement," including its relationship to the democratic movement. Her approach is to examine these issues in the context of feminists' understanding of the Russian Revolution, gained through the writings of Li Dazhao and Yamakawa Kikue.

Two essays on women's history appeared in the journal *Chūgoku kindai shi kenkyūkai tsūshin* 15-16: Satō Akiko, "A Study of Women Laborers in the Silk Industry in Shanghai in the First Half of the 1920's"[a]; and Maeyama Kanako, "Yang Changji and Women's Liberation in Hunan: A Translation of His *Jiehun lun* (On Marriage) and a Look at His 'Notes on the Reform of the Family System.'"[a] While Satō analyzes the strikes and struggles of Chinese women workers in silk mills, Maede discusses the influence exerted by Yang Changji on the women's liberation movement.

Kubota Hiroko's study, "A Draft of a Brief Chronological Biography of Song Qingling"[a] (*Shingai kakumei kenkyū* 3), diligently traces the activities of woman revolutionary Song Qingling. We also a have book that discusses women's issues from the Taiping Rebellion through the May Fourth era: Nakayama Yoshihiro, *Kindai Chūgoku ni okeru josei kaihō no shisō to kōdō* (Women's Liberation in Thought and Action in Modern China).[a] This volume has been reviewed by Ono Kazuko in *Chūgoku kenkyū geppō* (429).

Among articles adopting the tools of social history are: Ōno Miboko, "The Formation and Development of the Shanghai Theater"[a] (*Ochanomizu shigaku* 26-27); and Kurahashi Masanao, "The Trial of the Dongshenghe Company in Yingkou: An Example of Commercial Adjudication in the Late Qing"[a] (*Rekishigaku kenkyū* 517). Ōno traces the emergence and growth of the theater as it reflects the development of the city of Shanghai itself, and she analyzes the characteristics of the theater there as well as the reasons for its development. Kurahashi's essay on the commercial trial over the bankruptcy of the great merchant house of Dongshenghe, in the trading port of Yingkou in northeast China, throws light on the reforms in the legal system during the Guangxu reign as well as on the growth of the city of Yingkou.

In the field of popular movements, considerable scholarly attention focused on issues from the Taiping era. Namiki Yorihisa's essay, "The Rent Resistance Rebellion of the *lianzhuanghui* in Henan in the 1850's (Part 2)"[b] (*Chūgoku kindai shi kenkyū* 3),[2] looks at the *lianzhuanghui* of Henan Province which was organized as a *tuanlian* for village self-defense in the face of the Taiping army's northern expedition. It eventually sought reductions in the land tax burden and undertook a struggle for rent resistance. However, under official pressures it "split apart." Namiki points out that within the *lianzhuanghui* there was an "opposition between those who sought the maintenance of the local village social order and those aimed at its disintegration."

Meguro Katsuhiko discusses the Hunan "braves" who were organized to crush the Taipings in his essay "The Relationship Between *Tuanlian* and Local Braves: The Case of the Hunan *Tuanlian* and the Hunan Braves"[a] (*Aichi kyōiku daigaku kenkyū hōkoku* 32).

Natsui Haruki's article, "On Rule by Local Bullies in Suzhou During the Taiping Period: The Case of Xu Zhu of Yongchang, Changzhou County"[a] (in *Masubuchi*), analyzes the control exercised by a kinsman of Xu Peiyuan, a landlord who had submitted to the Taipings. He notes that Mr. Xu held local power, semi-independent of both the Taipings and the Qing state.

Sasaki Masaya's essay, "Addenda to Missionary Cases in Youyang (Part 1)"[b] (*Kindai Chūgoku* 13), makes use of new historical materials to examine the raids on missionary schools by *tuanlian* in the Youyang region of Sichuan and the resistance of missionaries to them. These raids were organized by landlords and rich merchants in preparation for the approach of Shi Dakai's army.

A. F. Lindley's book (translated by Kojima Shinji, with an explanatory note), *The Taeping as they are, by one of them* [London, 1864] (Part 1)[a]

(*Rōhyakusei no sekai* 1), introduces and translates Lindley's observations of the Taipings when he joined the army of Li Xiucheng.

I have written three essays on the Taipings: "The Chiangchuan Group from the Taihu Region of Jiangsu and Zhejiang during the Taiping Revolutionary Era"[a] (in *Masubuchi*); "The Chiangchuan Group in the Areas Occupied by the Taipings: The Taihu Region"[b] (*Rekishigaku kenkyū* 522); and "The Chiangchuan Group After the Suppression of the Taipings"[c] (*Hitotsubashi ronsō* 85.1). In these articles, I clarify the situation behind the formation, growth, decline, and revival of the Chiangchuan group, an armed force mostly of unemployed who acted in concert with the Taiping army during their advance into and occupation of Jiangsu and Zhejiang. I try to reinterpret the Taipings from the perspective of village society, and I describe the relationship between the local Taiping army of occupation and the forces of Sun Jinpiao and Fei Yucheng. What remains to be done is an analysis of the relationship of the landlord system to each of these levels.

One article dealing with popular movements after the Taiping Rebellion is Noguchi Tetsurō, "The Red Lotus Sect and the Gelaohui"[a] (*Tōyōshi kenkyū* 42.2). He discusses the relationship between these two groups in the Tongzhi reign by examining the leadership, religious precepts, and membership of the Red Lotus Sect, focusing on their activities in Yining Department [Jiangsi], Liuyang County [Hunan], and elsewhere in the province of Jiangsi.

We have two essays by Katō Naoko: "Currency Problems in the Early Republic: A Look at Shandong After the First World War"[a] (*Shingai kakumei kenkyū* 3); and "On the Movement Opposing Civil Government in Shandong"[b] (*Ochanomizu joshi daigaku jimbun kagaku kiyō* 36). Each of these two essays in its own way examines Japan's purchase of official Chinese currency in Shandong after World War I and the local resistance and opposition to the installation of a civil government.

Let us now turn to articles dealing with international relations. First, Nagano Shin'ichirō's essay, "The Parliamentary Debates in England Surrounding the Arrow Incident"[a] (*Daitō bunka daigaku keizai ronshū* 35), discusses the significance of the Arrow Incident from the British perspective and clarifies the details of their armed intervention against the Taipings.

Katō Yūzō has written a four-part essay entitled: "The World Around the Time of the Black Ships (1): The Arrival of Perry's Squadron"[a]; "(2): The Background to Perry's Expedition"[b]; "(3): The People Surrounding Perry"[c]; and "(4): England and America in East Asia"[d] (*Shisō* 709-711, 713). Through the medium of Commodore Perry's "Black Ships," Katō attempts to describe the three-sided relations between Japan, China, and the West (Europe and the United States) in the context of world history. More segments of this long essay are expected.

In his article, "The Japanese Shipping Industry During the Formative Period of Imperialism: The Establishment of an East Asian Trading Network After the Russo-Japanese War"[a] (*Shigaku zasshi* 92.10), Kokaze Hidemasa describes the advance of Japanese shipping companies into East Asian waters.

Yamane Yukio's essay, "The Twenty-One Demands and the Responses of Japanese"[b] (in *Sakuma*), introduces Japanese arguments of agreement, opposition, and discontent over the Twenty-One Demands and the negotiations with China.

Two essays deal with Japanese rule in Taiwan: Mukōyama Hiroo, "Law and Politics in Taiwan Under Japanese Rule: From the Viewpoint of Native Jurisprudence"[a] (*Kokugakuin hōgaku* 21.2); and Wakabayashi Masahiro, "The [Japanese] Governor-General's Regime and the Indigenous Landholding Class in Taiwan: On the Founding of the Taizhong Public Middle School, 1912-1915"[a] (*Ajia kenkyū* 29.4). These two pieces deal, respectively, with issues of native jurisprudence and with the anti-Japanese movement in Taiwan. In addition, Wakabayashi has written a volume covering a variety of issues in modern Taiwanese history, *Taiwan kō-Nichi undō shi kenkyū* (A Study of the History of the Anti-Japanese Movement in Taiwan).[b] This book still awaits review.

Nakamura Takashi's article, "People Registered in Taiwan from Fuzhou: 1909"[a] (*Nampō bunka* 10), introduces materials concerning the issue of "people registered as living in Taiwan" after the Japanese occupation began there. Christian Daniels' essay, "The Sugar Industry and Merchant Capital in Southern Taiwan in the Late Qing, 1870-1895"[a] (*Tōyō gakuhō* 64.3-4), offers an analysis of the management structure of the sugar industry of Taiwan after the industry had become incorporated into world markets. Mitsushima Toku discusses issues concerning national borders in his "Governing the Sichuan Borders in the Late Qing and the Sichuan Army's Entry into Tibet"[a] (*Taga*).

Finally, we have a number a books to mention, each deserving reviews of their own: Nagai Kazumi, *Chūgoku kindai seiji shi ronsō* (Studies in the Political History of Modern China);[a] Usui Katsumi, *Chūgoku o meguru kindai Nihon gaikō* (Modern Japanese Diplomacy Concerning China);[a] Liu Mingxiu, *Taiwan tōji to ahen mondai* (Control over Taiwan and the Opium Question);[a] Chūgoku shi kenkyūkai (Chinese history study group), ed., *Chūgoku shi zō no saikōsei: kokka to nōmin* (A Reconstruction of the Image of Chinese History: The State and the Peasantry);[a] Imahori Seiji, ed., *Chūgoku e no apurōchi, sono rekishi teki tenkai* (The Historical Development of Approaches to China);[a] and Nishimura Kōjirō, ed. and trans., *Chūgoku ni okeru hō no keishōsei ronsō* (Debates on the Nature of Legal Inheritance in China).[a]

I would also like to point out two new valuable guides to research based on recent work in East Asian history: Yamane Yukio, ed., *Chūgoku shi kenkyū nyūmon* (Introduction to the Study of Chinese History, 2 vol.);[c] and the first three of a projected five-volume work edited by Shimada Kenji, *Ajia rekishi kenkyū nyūmon* (Introduction to the Study of Asian History).[a]

3

Ming-Qing Studies in Japan: 1984

Ishibashi Takao, in *Shigaku zasshi*
94.5 (May 1985), 218-225.

Until recently many studies in Ming and Qing history have been concerned with trying to elucidate social and economic processes of development in land relations. This has led to a thinning in the ranks of scholars in fields other than social and economic history and to an ossification of other research topics. The Qing dynasty has generally been seen both as an alien conquest dynasty and as the last native, "Chinese-style" autocratic dynasty in an agricultural society. Although the Qing did have this dual quality, few have examined the issue comprehensively. It would be no exaggeration to say that the two sides have been severed and researched independently. The tendency to treat the period before the Manchus entered China separately from the period after, and the fact that few scholars have examined the eight *gūsa* (banners) system of banner lands and imperial villas as research subjects in social and economic history, provide but one reflection of this problem.

In reviewing the over 120 books and articles from last year, I see no radical change in this situation. Yet, in looking for new points of view and issues, we should pay particular attention to the publication of several symposia. I begin with these.

Symposia

The volume, *Chūgoku Kōnan no inasaku bunka, sono gakujutsu teki kenkyū* (The Culture of Rice Cultivation in Jiangnan, Interdisciplinary Studies),[a] edited by Watanabe Tadase and Sakurai Yumio, represents the record of the "Jiangnan Delta Symposium" held in July 1977 at the Southeast Asia Research Center of Kyoto University. Using natural science and relying on field work, the papers at the symposium raised criticisms of the theories of East Asian scholars who have based their work concerning the opening of the Jiangnan delta solely on written records. The collected essays from the conference are:

(1) "On *huogeng shuinou*[1]: Early Reclamation of the Delta,"

(2) "On Polder Lands (*yutian*) and Enclosed Lands (*weitian*) in the Song and Yuan: Technological Responses to Reclamation of the Delta,"

(3) "On Champa Rice Cultivation: Agricultural Responses to Reclamation of the Delta,"

(4) "On Polder Divisions (*fenyu*)^2 in the Ming and Qing: Diversification in the Reclamation of the Delta,"

(5) "The Development of Cash Crops,"

(6) "Jiangnan Agriculture and Japan."

The last two chapters are of direct concern to Ming and Qing studies. Two debates that arose at the symposium involved polder differentiation (as it concerned water control practices when water control communities were reorganized) and rice, cotton, and mulberry cultivation (as they concerned rural handicrafts and commercial produce). This book should be analyzed in its entirety, and I shall leave that to separate reviews.

Kyūshū University's Department of East Asian History published *Sen kyūhyaku hachijūsan nen, Chūgoku shi shinpojium, Gen-Min-Shin ki ni okeru kokka "shihai" to minshūzō no saitentō, "shihai" no Chūgoku teki tokushitsu* (1983 Symposium on Chinese History, a Reinvestigation of State "Control" and the Image of the People in Yuan, Ming, and Qing Times, the Distinctive Nature of Chinese "Control").[a] This volume is the report of a symposium convened in July 1983, and it followed two other conferences: "Problems Concerning Rent Resistance Struggles"[a] (held in 1980 at Hokkaidō University, Department of East Asian History), and "The Perspective of Local Society: Local Society and Leadership"[a] (held in 1981 at Nagoya University, Department of East Asian History). According to the report of the Kyūshū conference, past studies of "the state and the people" have tended to ignore the rich historical image that society at a given time possesses by rendering in a monistic fashion the relationship between "state control and the controlled." The Kyūshū conference aimed at reexamining this phenomenon.

This conference volume has two parts: "Understanding State 'Control' in the Yuan, Ming, and Qing Periods" and "Social Relations among the People and State 'Control' in the Yuan, Ming, and Qing Periods." The first part includes the following essays:

(1) Katayama Tomoo, "On Scholars in the Yuan Era,"[a]

(2) Ido Kazutada, "On the Imperial Bodyguard in the Yuan: Military Structure and Military Officials,"[a]

(3) Wada Masahiro, "The Examination System in the Ming Dynasty and the Literati,"[a]

(4) Shiroi Takashi, "Political Factions in the Wanli Period and the Literati: On the Ministry of Personnel in the Wanli 20's [1592-1601],"[a] and

(5) Ōtani Toshio, "Qing Political Structure and the Literati."[c]

The second part includes:

(1) Sōda Hiroshi, "Establishment Ideology and Popular Thought in the

Ming Dynasty,"[b]
(2) Asai Motoi, "Religious Societies and the People in the Ming and Qing,"[a]
(3) Watanabe Atsushi, "Secret Societies and the People in the Qing Dynasty in the Lower Yangzi Delta,"[a]
(4) Kanbe Teruo, "Understanding Minority Ethnic Groups,"[a]
(5) Kishi Kazuyuki, "The Image of Vagrants in Local Guangdong Society in the Pearl River Basin at the End of the Ming,"[a]
(6) Kawakatsu Mamoru, "The Politics of Subofficial Functionaries in the Ming and Qing and the People."[a]
One of the hallmarks of this symposium was that the authors ignored the problems of rural villages and peasants, and they counterposed the literati against those "ordinately distinctive, extreme elements," (p. 214) such as vagrants and religious secret societies. At the same time, they tried to interpret the Yuan, Ming, and Qing as one era. Two reasons for fixing this as a single period are: "because of such things as the establishment of the province as an administrative unit, the founding of the capital in Beijing, the presentation of ministers from many foreign states, and the succession of administrative regulations like the *Yuan dianzhang*, all from the Yuan dynasty on" (p. 259); and "because conditions continued to emerge making it impossible to ignore the existence of non-Han ethnic groups in structuring an image of Chinese society as a whole" (p. 253). However, the periodization suggested by this book is based on issues of concern primarily to the literati. It should be noted that this way of understanding the Yuan, Ming, and Qing was attempted some fifteen years ago from a different perspective. An example would be: Ishibashi Hideo, "On the Qing, a Conquest Dynasty"[a] (*Sekai shi no kenkyū* 54 [1968]); and Ishibashi Hideo, "The Great Yuan, the Great Ming, the Great Qing: China and the Five Ethnic Groups"[b] (*Sekai shi no kenkyū* 63 [1970]).[3]

Political, Military, and Legal History

Two articles concerned the early Ming. Matsumoto Takaharu's "The Circumstances Surrounding the Establishment of the Capital in the Ming"[a] (*Tōhōgaku* 67) examines the founding of the capital by Ming Taizu. Wataru Masahiro's "The Special Civil Service Recruitment in the Hongwu Reign of the Ming Dynasty"[a] (*Rekishi* 63) investigates the background, aims, and methods of the special recruitment [for the civil service "by decree," outside the regular procedures of the examination system][4] in the early Hongwu years. An essay concerned with examination officials, Wada Masahiro's "An Investigation of the Succession of Family Pedigree among Ming Examination Officials"[b] (*Seinan gakuin daigaku bunri ronshū* 24.1), analyzes generational differences in the number of officials recruited and the actual applica-

tion of the privileged exemption from labor service in the Ming.
We have two essays on the *weiso* [Guards and Battalions] system in the early Ming. Kawagoe Yasuhiro's "Circumstances Surrounding Arrival at a Post for *weiso* Officials in the Ming Dynasty: The Case of the Yulin Guard"[a] (in *Okamoto*) examines the arrival of each new *weiso* official at Yulin on the basis of each's family registers (*weixuanfu*).

Kusunoki Kendō's "Control over Liaodong in the Ming Period and the Sanwan Guard: On Jurchen Military Officials in the Early Ming"[a] (*Shikyō* 9) makes use of the family registers of Sanwan Guard officials to examine the process by which Jurchens who had submitted to the Ming were reorganized into the Sanwan Guard in Liaodong. He also tries to analyze the structure of the Sanwan Guard and the actual nature of the Jurchen military officials there. Kusunoki cites two passages from the *Ming shilu* (Veritable Records of the Ming Dynasty): "They ordered the establishment of the two *cheng* [walled settlements or towns—JAF] of Zizai and Kuaihuo in Liaodong, and the creation of the two subprefectures of Zizai and Anle;" and "They additionally created the two subprefectures of Zizai and Anle in Liaodong." He argues from these citations that the "Ming court set up the two *cheng* of Zizai and Kuaihuo as an example of its acceptance of Jurchens who had submitted to it, but the administrative unit of a *cheng* did not exist in the Ming.... In order to control these Jurchens, after having installed these two *cheng*, they set up within each *cheng* the civil administrative organ of the subprefecture" (p. 22). I believe what the text actually means is that because these Jurchens had submitted to the court, the court used the Jurchens' residential areas (known as *hoton*) to "additionally create" subprefectures in each region; and it conferred jurisdiction upon them in these two *hoton*. Furthermore, I have my doubts that the difference between Jurchens not resident in Anle subprefecture and the Jurchens who resided in Anle and Zizai subprefectures was an issue solely of sinification, as Kusunoki argues.

In his essay "The Financial Base of Li Chengliang's Power (Part 1)"[c] (*Seinan gakuin daigaku bunri ronshū* 25.1), Wada Masahiro analyzes the military and financial strength of Li Chengliang, Regional Commander of the Liaodong defense command (*zhen*) in the Wanli period. Li, who was known for many military exploits and for his corrupt activities at court, is one illustration of the decadent structure of the military administration in Liaodong in the late Ming. Further pieces on this subject are expected from Wada.

In his essay "On the *Yang Wenruo xiansheng ji*, Concerning the Views of Zhang Xianqing"[b] (*Tōyō gakuhō* 65.3-4), Yoshio Hiroshi argues for the necessity of studying the political history of the central government during the Chongzhen reign at the end of the Ming. He uses the memorials in the literary collection of Yang Sichang, who planned to establish additional taxes in the Chongzhen reign period, to demonstrate their value as historical materials.

Fukumoto Masakazu's book *Minmatsu Shinsho* (The Late Ming and Early Qing),[a] is a collection of eighteen essays originally published between 1961 and 1984. Using literary methods, he tries to understand the situation of historical actors in the late Ming and early Qing.

Another essay on the early Qing is Matsuura Shigeru's "The System of Hereditary Officials in the Tianming Era"[a] (*Tōyō shi kenkyū* 42.4). Investigating hereditary officials who have scarcely been treated by specialists heretofore, Matsuura examines their relationship with the eight banners system during the reign of Emperor Taizu. By considering "military officials" as "hereditary officials" and contrasting them with "eight banners officials," he tries to "separate conceptually the system of hereditary officials from the eight banners system" (p. 123). However, he seems to have confused official posts (*guan*) with hereditary positions (*zhi*) here. The first thing we have to do is to distinguish carefully between peerage rank, official post, and hereditary position. Furthermore, confusion may be the result of differences in vocabulary used in source materials; for example, there is the problem of seeing *amban*, *amba janggin*, and *amban janggin* as all the same.

Ishibashi Hideo has written two essays along these lines: "A Short Study of the Qing Dynasty: A Look at the Eight Banners System (Part 1)"[c] (*Sekai shi no kenkyū* 118); and "*Aha* in the Early Qing, Particularly in the Reign of Taizu"[d] (*Eikyōshū* 1). The first of these examines problems of terminology concerning the eight banners system within the context of political changes of the early Qing. The second is part of a longer analysis of the three terms: *irgen, jusen,* and *aha.* This segment deals with *aha* during the reign of Taizu.

Hosoya Yoshio's article, "A Reinvestigation of the Rebellion of the Three Feudatories: The Activities of Shang Kexi's Descendants"[a] (*Tōhoku daigaku Tōyōshi ronshū* 1) shows that the rebellion of one of the three feudatories, that of Shang Kexi, was a fabrication, used by the Qing to dismantle Shang's satrapy. He calls into question the whole meaning of the "Rebellion of the Three Feudatories."

In my essay "An Annotated Translation of the Secret Memorials of Gioroi Mamboo Concerning Taiwan in the *Gongzhong dang'an Kangxi chao zouzhe*"[b] (*Chūgoku kindai shi kenkyū* 4), I transcribe into Roman letters fifty-four Manchu language memorials of Gioroi Mamboo, who served as Governor of Fujian from 1711 and Governor-General of Fujian and Zhejiang from 1715. I also provide an annotated Japanese translation and an analysis.

Sakuma Shigeo's article, "On Tang Ying, the Supervisor of the Government Pottery Works at Jingdezhen"[a] (*Shiyū* 16), examines the production of ceramics through the biography of Tang Ying. He equates a Supervisor-in-Chief of the Imperial Household Department (*neiwufu zongguan*) with Grand Minister of the Imperial Household Department (*neidachen*) which will invite confusion. The former was the Manchu *booi amban*, and the latter was the *dorgi amban*.

In his essay "North and South in Local Government under the Qing"[a] (in *Chūgoku bunka*), Narakino Shimesu attempts a cultural comparison between North China and various places in the South, by examining how local governments in the Qing coped with various problems.

In his article "A Study of the *Changsui lun*: One Historical Source on *changsui*"[a] (in *Nishijima*), Saeki Yūichi introduces a volume from the collection of Professor Niida Noboru. He also studies *changsui*[5] who, together with private secretaries and subofficial functionaries, were in charge of the administration of local government.

Concerning legal history, we have a volume by Shiga Shūzō, *Shindai Chūgoku no hō to saiban* (Chinese Law and Courts in the Qing Dynasty).[a] The entire book deserves a full-length review. Its contents are as follows:

(1) Criminal Courts in the Qing Period: Their Administrative Nature;

(2) Murder as the Private Punishment of Clans, as It Appears in Criminal Cases: A Response to National Law;

(3) The Lack of the Concept of the Decisive Authority of Legal Judgment, Particularly in Civil Cases;

(4) A General Analysis of the Sources of Legal Authority: Law, Reason, Circumstances;[6]

(5) The Classics, Rites, and Customs as the Origins of Law;

(6) Appendix: Complicity in the Tang Legal Code.

Taxation Systems

In his essay, "Fishing Tax Offices and Fishermen in The Ming Dynasty"[a] (*Chūō daigaku bungakubu kiyō* 112), Nakamura Jihee analyzes problems concerning the fishing industry and fishermen through the offices which levied taxes on them.

Satō Manabu argues on behalf of the need for research on urban society in the history of the land tax and labor service systems. His essay, "The Labor Service and Its Conversion to Silver Payment among Beijing Shopkeepers during the Ming"[b] (*Rekishi* 62), analyzes the process through which labor service for shopkeepers (principally in Beijing and Tongzhou) assessed on urban commerce and industry was converted to payment in silver. He examines urban commerce and industry as well as the state's understanding of them at the time.

In her essay "The Single Whip Law in Shandong Province during the Ming Dynasty"[a] (in *Nishijima*), Ōkuma Akiko investigates the first implementation of the Single Whip law in Shandong, pointing out that it was aimed at limiting the special privileges of the literati. Kōsaka Masanori's article, "A Study of the Xushu Tax Collection Station in the Qing Era (Part

4): Xushu and the Circulation of Commodities"[a] (*Tōhoku gakuin daigaku ronshū* 14), examines the collection of taxes through customs collections (*zhengke*) and forcible seizure by non-governmental agents (*baila*).

Landownership

In his essay, "A Visit to the Fish-Scale Registers: A Study Trip to China"[a] (*Kindai Chūgoku kenkyū ihō* 6), Tsurumi Naohiro introduces the fish-scale registers in the collection of the Historical Research Institute of the Chinese Academy of Social Sciences. Oyama Masaaki makes a cumulative analysis of materials that have been used in China thus far relating to slaves and bond-servants in his article, "The Slave and Bondservant Systems in Huizhou Prefecture in the Ming and Qing, as Seen from Documentary Sources"[a] (in *Nishijima*), the first part of a long work in progress. Fujii Hiroshi has completed Part 10 of his long and still unfinished essay, "The Basic Structure of the One-Field Two-Owners System"[a] (*Kindai Chūgoku* 15). This part concerns "*Dingshou* and Surface Rights."

Hamashima Atsutoshi has written two essays: "Prisons in the Coastal Provinces of Southeast China at the End of the Ming"[c] (in *Nishijima*); and "Local Jails in China during the Ming and Qing Eras: A Preliminary Study"[d] (*Hōsei shi kenkyū* 33). Both of these essays examine the *pu* and *cang*, which were new varieties of local jails that emerged at the end of the Ming to enforce the collection of rent from tenant farmers. The former piece looks primarily at the formation of *pu* and *cang* in Fujian and Guangdong; and the latter adds a functional perspective by investigating the *pu* of Jiang-nan, the *cang* of North China, and the *cang* of Central and South China.

Morita Shigemitsu's book, *Shindai tochi shoyūkenhō kenkyū* (Studies in the Landownership Laws of the Qing Dynasty),[a] offers a structural analysis of property rights by looking at official lands, garrison lands, banner lands, and particularly private lands. The book has three parts:
(1) The Land System;
(2) Authentification of Property Rights;
(3) Judicial Protection of Property Rights.
We await reviews of the entire book.

In his article "Contradictions and Their Reform in the *tujia* System in the Pearl River Delta of Guangdong at the End of the Qing (Shunde County, Xiangshan County)"[d] (*Chūgoku kindai shi kenkyū* 4), Katayama Tsuyoshi moves from his earlier work on Nanhai County to examine Shunde and Xiangshan Counties. While considering the shift of the *tujia* system in Shunde and Nanhai to the form of *laohu/ding* [nominal landowner responsible for tax payment and real landowner-JAF], he points out that the case of Xiangshan County, where the *dayi* disappeared, possesses major significance.[7]

Okuzaki Yūji's essay, "Landlord-Tenant Relations in the Late Qing: An Investigation of Cases from Morality Books"[b] (*Aoyama shigaku* 8), examines thirteen cases from the Daoguang and Xianfeng periods as seen in the *Zhunyu lunke jiyao*. Hosokawa Kazutoshi, in his article "Landowner Mentality and Human Relations in Chinese Villages, as Seen by *Zhongren*"[a] (*Hirosaki daigaku jimbun gakubu bunkei ronsō* 19.3), analyzes contractual documents from Jiangsu and Zhejiang. He offers a reexamination of the functions, status, and appellations of *zhongren* (intermediaries) as seen in the *Chūgoku nōson kankō chōsa* (Investigation of Village Customs and Practices in China).[8]

Commodity Production Relations

In his article, "Society and Famine Relief in the Jiangnan Delta in the Late Ming"[b] (in *Nishijima*), Kawakatsu Mamoru investigates the government's efforts at famine relief. He looks particularly at the rise of cash crops, the social transformation involving urbanization, and the flow of rice in the middle and lower reaches of the Yangzi River. He also points out that we can see the social context of this relief in the stress placed on the official control over rice.

One essay that deals with policies concerning rice requirements in Guangdong is Matsuda Yoshirō's "Fluctuations in the Prices of Rice and the Regulation of Rice Needs in Guangzhou Prefecture, Guangdong: Late Ming to Mid-Qing"[a] (*Chūgoku shi kenkyū* 8). Tanaka Masatoshi's essay, "On Advance Payment Production in the Wholesale System of the Ming and Qing Periods: Notes Concerning the History of Research into Cloth Production"[a] (in *Nishijima*) reviews the history of scholarship on production financed by advance payment from wholesalers. In addition he examines the establishment and the significance of this system of production with examples drawn primarily from wholesalers, textile piece-workers, and the heads of calendering factories. Hayashi Kazuo's article, "The Development of Local Cities in Early Modern China: The Case of Wuqing Garrison in the Taihu Plain"[a] (in *Chūgoku kinsei*), examines the growth of a garrison town at a junction of commercial transport, with cases from the Song, Ming, and Qing eras.

Water Control Relations

Shiba Yoshinobu's essay, "On the *Maji gai ba wei qiao shimo ji*"[a] (in *Nishijima*), examines the last ten centuries of change in the organization of water control around the Maji dam in northern Zhejiang. His basic source is the one named in the title of the article. In another essay, "The *Xianghu shuili zhi* and the *Xianghu kaolüe*: Water Control Management in Lake Xiang of Xiaoshan County, Zhejiang"[b] (in *Satō*), Shiba looks at the two historical sources (cited in his title) which concern Lake Xiang (Xiaoshan County, Shaoxing Prefecture). He investigates the formation, history, and organization of the lake's water control system from the Song dynasty forward.

Kitada Hidebito's essay, *"Wu* and Settlers Along the Boundaries of Lake Tai in China"[a] (*Shihō* 17), goes back as far as the 8th century to examine the *wu* (fortified settlements) that were formed in these mountainous regions.

Morita Akira has written three articles: "Liu Guangfu and the *Jingye guiluüe* in the Late Ming"[a] (*Kōgakkan ronsō* 17.1); "A Study of Water Control in the Zhedong Region at the End of the Ming Dynasty"[b] (*Shigaku kenkyū* 165); and "Dredging Work in Changzhou during the Qing Dynasty"[c] (in *Satō*). The first of these demonstrates the value of the *Jingye guilüe* as a historical source. The second piece analyzes the management regulations for solving problems of water usage in the Zhuji region of Zhedong, based on the source described in the previous essay. The third article looks at the supervision of waterworks within the city of Changzhou.

A number of articles examine water control outside Jiangnan. Tani Mitsutaka's "The Confluence of the Yellow and Huai Rivers and the River Conservancy Work of Yang Yikui"[a] (in *Satō*) takes a penetrating look at Yang's work. Yoshioka Yoshinobu, in his essay "On Water Control in Ningxia during the Ming Dynasty"[a] (in *Satō*), examines the structure of water usage in the Ningxia plain along the middle reaches of the Yellow River. In his piece, "On Water Disputes in Shanxi during the Modern Era"[a] (in *Satō*), Yoshinami Kōji conceptualizes the relationship between the organization of water control and the village by looking specifically at water disputes over the northern and southern canals of the four Jinshui canals in the Taiyuan region. Matsuda Yoshirō's "Water Control Projects in North-central Taiwan during the Qing and the Formative Process of the One-Field Two-Owners System"[b] (in *Satō*) looks at water control in Taiwan in the Qing period. Finally, Hori Tadashi, in his essay "Notes on Water Sources in Chinese Turkestan, an Examination of the 'Treatise on Drainage Ditches' of the *Xinjiang tuzhi*"[a] (in *Satō*), focuses on the water control projects and the sources of water in various locales in Xinjiang under the Qing.

In addition, we should note an essay my Ueda Makoto, "Locality and Clan: The Mountainous Region of Zhejiang"[b] (*Tōyō bunka kenkyūjo kiyō* 94). He touches on the role of clan cohesion and local society in water control and landownership, examining three prefectures in Zhejiang Province: Quzhou, Jinhua, and Shaoxing.

Intellectual History

In his essay "Fang Xiaoru's Political Thought: An Idealized Conception of the Sovereign in the Early Ming"[b] (*Sakai joshi tanki daigaku kiyō* 19), Danjō

Hiroshi examines Fang Xiaoru's promotion of a revivalist policy for the Jianwen Emperor. He looks at Fang's political thought through his views on the sovereign, the legal system, and the well-field system.

One article concerned with literati in the Qing dynasty is Miura Hideichi's "Tang Bin and Long Longqi: Human Understanding and Statecraft Consciousness among Literati in the Early Qing"[a] (*Bunka* 48.1-2). Miura offers a comparative analysis of the thought of these two men who attained leadership positions, respectively, in the Zhu Xi and Wang Yangming schools.

Kawata Teiichi's essay, "Literati and Evidential Research in the Qianlong and Jiaqing Periods: Yuan Mei, Sun Xingyan, Dai Zhen, and Zhang Xuecheng"[a] (*Tōyōshi kenkyū* 42.4), looks primarily at the intellectual trends among literati in the Qianlong and Jiaqing eras.

Ōtani Toshio's "Sovereign Power in the Qing Dynasty and the Literati"[d] (*Jimbun gakka ronshū* 19) raises the issue of monarchical despotism and the autonomous power of literati in conflicts over statecraft and aiding the people. He provides a comparative examination of the Yongzheng period and the 1898 Reform Movement at the end of the Qing.

Araki Kengo's book *Yōmeigaku no kaiten to Bukkyō* (The Development of the Wang Yang-ming School and Buddhism)[a] deserves a separate review.

Class Struggle, Religion, and Ethnic Minorities

Sanada Takehiko's essay, "On the Rebellion of Lan Tingduan in the Zhengde Period of the Ming Dynasty"[a] (*Tōyō daigaku Tōyō shi kenkyū hōkoku* 3), examines the uprising of Lan Tingduan in Sichuan Province during the Zhengde reign.

On "Japanese" pirates (Ch., *wokou*; J., *wakō*) during the Jiajing era of the Ming, Itō Kimio has written "Trends and Problems in Chinese Historical Research on the History of Japanese Pirates during the Jiajing Period"[a] (*Shigaku* 53.4). He examines developments in Chinese research.

Taniguchi Fusao's essay, "The Suppression of Pirate Rebellions in the Jiajing Period and Washi furen"[a] (*Tōyō daigaku bungakubu kiyō* 37), examines conditions of local officials and local chiefs [in aboriginal areas—JAF] in Tianzhou Prefecture, with special reference to one "Washi furen," the wife of an official by the name of Chen Meng sent to govern an aboriginal area. She was active in putting down a local uprising.

An article by the Chinese scholar Wang Lianmao (trans. Miki Satoshi), "Rent Theft in Quanzhou in the Late Ming and the Struggles of the Doulaohui"[a] (*Shihō* 17), concerns the Doulaohui which became active during the Chongzhen reign period.

Concerning Buddhism, we have an essay by Noguchi Yoshitaka, "On Huang Duanbo, Buddhist Layman of the Late Ming"[a] (*Tetsugaku nempō* 43). He discusses Huang Duanbo who is considered to stand at the intersection of the two Buddhist sects of Linji and Tsaodong.

Kuzudani Noboru's article, "How Catholics Preserved the Faith during the Religious Troubles in Nanjing at the End of the Ming"[a] (*Hitotsubashi ronsō* 92.1), looks at Catholicism in the late Ming and examines its oppression and the logic of those who kept the faith.

One essay that concerns the White Lotus sect in the Jiaqing period of the Qing dynasty is Watanabe Atsushi's "The Reform of the Salt Administration in Hedong and the White Lotus Rebellion"[b] (in *Tanaka*). He examines reforms in the salt administration in the Hedong circuit within the context of salt reforms from the late Qianlong through the Jiaqing eras, and he draws links between these reforms and the White Lotus Rebellion.

Terada Takanobu's article, "A Discussion of Muslims in Quanzhou in the Ming Dynasty"[a] (*Tōyō shi kenkyū* 42.4), aims primarily at introducing a collection of genealogical records on Muslims from Quanzhou.

Enoki Kazuo's essay, "The Establishment of Xinjiang as a Province (2 Parts): Central Asia in the 20th Century"[a] (*Kindai Chūgoku* 15, 16), investigates control over Xinjiang which began in the Qianlong period. He looks at Gong Zizhen, who suggested the creation of a provincial administration there in the Jiaqing period, and at the Jahangir expedition. Enoki expects to continue this essay with further installments.

Foreign Relations

In her essay "Tribute to the Court in the Yongle Period of the Ming"[b] (*MUSEUM* 398), Ōkuma Akiko continues her earlier work on the tribute system during the Hongwu reign. This time she looks at the Yongle era from the two perspectives of foreign policy and foreign trade.

Ikuta Shigeru has written two articles on the Ryūkyū Islands in the Ming: "The Ancient History of the Ryūkyū Islands from the Perspective of Foreign Relations: Toward an Understanding of the History of Rice Cultivation in the South Seas Islands"[a] (in *Nantō no inasaku bunka* [The Culture of Rice Cultivation in the Southern Islands],[a] ed. Ikuta and Watanabe Tadase); and "The Unification of the Three Kingdoms of the Ryūkyū Islands" (*Tōhō gakuhō* 65.3-4). The first of these describes Ryūkyū-Ming relations from 1372 until 1609 in the context of the political and economic structure of the Zhongshan Kingdom [of the Ryūkyūs]. In the second piece, he examines the unification of the three kingdoms which Shang Bazhi is said to have accomplished. He argues that this unification was in fact a legend created to support the centralization of power during the Shang Zhen period.

Maehira Fusaaki's essay, "An Investigation of the Ryūkyū Trade during the Period of Upheaval from Late Ming to Early Qing: On the Missions of the Kangxi Congratulatory Ships"[a] (*Kyūshū shigaku* 80), examines the missions of congratulatory tribute-bearing ships from the Ryūkyū Islands which honored the accession to the throne of the Kangxi emperor of the Qing dynasty. He looks at this from the perspective of Ryūkyūan domestic politics and trade. He also looks into the close relationship between the fiscal conditions of Satsuma and those of the Ryūkyūs, and into their hierarchical relationship within East Asia.

In his piece "The Development of Qing-Ryūkyū Relations from the Perspective of Political Culture"[a] (in *Okamoto*), Nagase Mamoru examines the tribute paid to the Qing by the Ryūkyū Islands. Since the Ryūkyūs were subservient both to the Qing dynasty and to Satsuma, he looks at this three-way relationship from the perspective of trade and diplomacy in East Asia.

Miyata Toshihiko's book *Ryūkyū Shinkoku kōeki shi* (The History of Ryūkyū-Qing Trade)[a] is based on the two collections of materials known as the *Lidai baoan*. He focuses on various problems involved in the hierarchical relations, tribute trade, and Ryūkyū-Qing relations. If we compare the original text as cited by Miyata with the photolithographed version in the original author's hand (printed by Taiwan University), numerous differences in characters, paragraphing, and emphasis can be pointed out. Although Miyata's work appears to have compared many manuscript editions, it probably would have been appropriate for him to have added some clarification where variant characters or supplementary material were used.

On tribute relations between the Ming and the Mongols, we have an essay by Shimada Masarō, "The Provisional Treaty between the Ming and the Tartars"[a] (*Hōritsu ronsō Meiji daigaku hōritsu kenkyūjo* 57.4). He discusses the treaty between the Ming and Altan Khan which concluded the peace negotiations in 1571, and he adds a point-by-point legal analysis of the main provisions for the Wanli reign years.

Enoki Kazuo's three-part work, "Macao in the Ming Dynasty"[b] (*Kikan Tōzai kōshō* 10-12), represents a translation of the work by an Italian merchant named Carletti who lived in Macao from 1598 to 1599, shortly after it was occupied by the Portuguese.

On relations between the Manchus and the Yi dynasty in Korea prior to the former's conquest of China, Morioka Yasu has written a two-part essay, "The Korean War Prisoner Trade after the Second Invasion of the Qing Army [into Korea]"[a] (*Chōsen gakuhō* 109; *Tōyō gakuhō* 65.1-2). He provides an analysis of the situation after 1639 concerning the ransom and return of prisoners during the Imjo reign.

Yoshida Kin'ichi's painstakingly detailed book, *Roshia no tōhō shinshutsu to Neruchinsuku jōyaku* (Russian Advances in the East and the Treaty of Nerchinsk),[a] deals with relations between the Qing and Russia. He focuses on the period from Sino-Russian contact at the beginning of the 17th century through the conclusion of the treaty in 1689, and he touches on the relations between the two countries after the peace negotiations. While reflecting on domestic conditions in the two countries, he elucidates their relations in great detail. We await well-deserved book reviews of this volume.

Literature

Ōki Yasushi's essay, "On the Authors and Readers of Vernacular Fiction in the Late Ming: A Rejoinder to the Views of Isobe Akira"[a] (*Mindai shi kenkyū* 12), points out that *shengyuan* were the principal readers supporting the rise of vernacular fiction late in the Ming dynasty.

For the Qing dynasty we have an essay by Lin Lianxiang (trans. and introduced by Furuda Shimahiro), "Disorders in the Examination System in Qing Period Fiction"[a] (*Hikaku bungaku kenkyū* 45). He analyzes the connections between the examination system and fiction.

Wang Xiaolian's article, "*Shenlou zhi*: A Pioneer Among Censured Novels in the Qing Dynasty"[a] (*Seinan gakuin daigaku bunri ronshū* 25.1), discusses the relationship between *Shenlou zhi*, *Honglou meng*, and *Jinpingmei* in historical background and significance.

In his essay, "The Intellectual Quality of Literature and the Historical Eye: Toward a Recognition of Asian History"[b] (*Rekishi hyōron* 409), Tanaka Masatoshi argues for a convergence between literary and historical studies.

In addition we have the following works: Kano Naoki, *Shinchō no seido to bungaku* (Qing Institutions and Literature)[a]; Hagio Chōichirō, "A Glossary for Old Chinese Vernacular Fiction and Drama (Part 15)"[a] (*Fukuoka daigaku sōgō kenkyūjohō* 79); and Kusaka Tsuneo and Kurahashi Yoshihiko, eds., *Nihon ni okeru Rō Sha kankei bunken mokuroku* (A Bibliography of Materials Concerning Lao She in Japan).[a]

Finally, I would like to note the publication of *State and Society in China: Japanese Perspectives on Ming-Qing Social and Economic History* (ed. Linda Grove and Christian Daniels, Tokyo, Tokyo University Press, 1984). The volume comprises English translations of ten essays (published between 1949 and 1976) concerning Ming and Qing history by Nishijima Sadao and others. It will be very important in widely introducing Japanese scholarship to foreign lands.

4

Japanese Studies of Post-Opium War China: 1984

Usui Sachiko and Kurihara Jun, in *Shigaku zasshi* 94.5 (May 1985), 225-234.

In response to the "Four Modernizations," there has been a noteworthy reassessment in contemporary China of the history of the modernization process in China prior to 1949. One particularly striking avenue of reassessment has been the new look at the early Westernization (*yangwu*) movement. For example, "A Preliminary Analysis of the Reasons for the Success or Failure of Capitalist Modernization in China and Japan in the Nineteenth Century"[a] (*Ritsumeikan hōgaku* 174) by Ding Richu and Du Xuncheng (trans. the research group on contemporary Chinese history under the direction of Ikeda Makoto) compares capitalist modernization in China and Japan and includes an analysis of why China developed later and more slowly than Japan. Related to this last point, Hata Korehito has written "Modern Chinese Scholarship on the Emergence of Chinese Capitalism"[a] (*Chūgoku kindai shi kenkyūkai tsūshin* 17).

By the same token, Japanese scholars have also recently begun to reevaluate the modern period in China, including the *yangwu* movement. While this may seem natural, in fact these new research trends in the two countries are not necessarily of the same character. Contemporary Chinese, laden with the weight of their own long history and in order to generate a new understanding of the past, have wanted to explain modernization, the rise of productive forces, and nationalism all as "good" and to locate their origins. By contrast, Japanese researchers have sought a perspective that places China within an international structure, not limited to a one-dimensional relationship between China and international capitalism or the powers. We have set out to consider anew what is "modern" in China by linking individual historical phenomena directly to historical stages, locating the genesis of class relations, reexamining methodology and avoiding evaluation, and understanding structural changes in China in modern times as a layered phenomenon.

Take, for example, an essay by Miyajima Hiroshi, "East Asia as Method:

On the Transition to Modernity in Three Nations of East Asia"[a] (*Rekishi hyōron* 412). While noting the limitations of "comparative modernization theory," Miyajima argues for a modern history of East Asia that unites an orientation toward capitalist modernization with the new world-systems approach.

While many scholars have noted the world historical links in the study of modern Chinese history, Kuroda Akinobu, in his "A Reevaluation of the Reform in Political Power in Modern China"[a] (*Rekishi hyōron* 412), notes two points: China has still not been stabilized through this linkage; and because we have failed to understand power in its structural relationship to social reproduction, we have not been able to come up with a theory of structural transformation.

On the other hand, in his essay "International Capitalism and Domestic Asian Capital"[a] (in *Shakai*), Hamashita Takeshi argues the necessity of an analytic perspective on "regional domestic capital in Asia" to elucidate one part of this larger problematic. In the articles to be discussed below, I would like to examine the results of the past year's scholarship according to various sub-fields.

On the issue of the penetration of foreign capital into Chinese markets, we have an essay by Motono Eiichi, "World Markets and the Trust Structure along the Middle and Lower Yangzi after the Arrow War"[a] (*Shigaku zasshi* 93.10). Motono points out that foreign firms and colonial banks in China, which had been in a disadvantageous position vis à vis Chinese markets, survived the crisis of 1866 and tried to establish control over compradors, native banks, and Chinese merchants. As he notes, though, the initiative in the import business was snatched from Chinese merchants in the inland treaty ports. The chop loan, hitherto seen as a means of gaining control over native banks, was in fact a countermeasure taken by colonial banks at a calculated loss to try and eliminate the non-honoring of banknotes by offering the native banks an advantage.

In "Urbanization and the Development of Capitalism in China"[c] (in *Shakai*), Shiba Yoshinobu addresses the advance of foreign merchants and banks into Chinese markets and the reasons why the Chinese were able to limit this. His analysis of the structure of Chinese markets offers useful clues. Although studies of Chinese market structure have thus far primarily addressed Ming and Qing history, we need research that advances the examination of structural changes in modern China over the long term. Nakamura Tetsuo's book, *Kindai Chūgoku shakai shi kenkyū josetsu* (An Introduction to Research into the History of Modern Chinese Society),[a] also analyzes the structure of Chinese society, including the structure of markets. This volume needs a separate review.

In addition, Morita Akira has written "Water Control in the Jiangnan

Delta in the Late Qing and Early Republic and Imperialist Control: The Establishment of the Huangpu River Authority in Shanghai"[a] (in *Tanaka*). He discusses the intervention of the foreign powers into the administration of waterways which can be seen in the founding of the "Huangpu River authority" (*junpuju*).

Five essays examine changes in the structure of power and control following the Taiping Rebellion: Natsui Haruki, "On Relations of Farm Rent Collection in Suzhou after the Taiping Rebellion: An Analysis of the Tax Registers"[a] (*Tochi seido shigaku* 103); Takahashi Kōsuke, "Benevolent Halls in Shanghai Early in the Modern Era: Their Response to 'Urban' Conditions"[a] (*Miyajiro kyōiku daigaku kiyō* 18.1); Takahashi Kōsuke, "One Perspective on Research into Benevolent Halls: Taking a Hint from the Benevolent Halls of Shanghai"[b] (*Chūgoku kindai shi kenkyūkai tsūshin* 17); Usui Sachiko, "Li Hongzhang's Countermeasures in Military Expenditure toward the End of the Taiping Rebellion"[a] (*Tōyō gakuhō* 65.3-4); and Sasaki Hiroshi, "On the Disciplined Forces"[a] (in *Okamoto*).

Natsui argues that the expropriation of tenants was exacerbated by the introduction of the payment of rent in currency as well as by the change from copper to nickel silver currency for such payments. While these changes were incorporated into the economic structure of the Chinese semi-colony, rent was collected through the utilization of the "powerful extra-economic coercion of public authority." This development, he argues, marked a transition in landlord-tenant relations from "private" to "public" relations.

In the first of his two essays, Takahashi claims that the large number of benevolent halls in Shanghai after the Taiping Rebellion was the result of the replacement of officials and others by "benevolent scholars" (*shanshi*) and "benevolent persons" (*shanren*). In the face of "urban" conditions, they acted to aid impoverished, neglected people. He argues that they obtained their funds from merchant capital, but that aid was aimed ultimately at sending these poor people back to their villages. In his second piece, Takahashi demonstrates that commercial capital from various quarters supported philanthropic work. He also argues that there are problems if we understand "benevolent contributions" (*shanjuan*), as we have in the past, only in the context of "tax collection and administration" by the "gentry" or the "gentry stratum" which stood to benefit landlords.

In my piece, I investigate changes in the structure of power through an examination of the financial policies of Li Hongzhang at the end of the Taiping Rebellion. I argue that the growing power in financial administration of governors-general vis à vis the center owed more to Governor Li Hongzhang's initiative in Jiangsu than it did to gentry initiative in local administrations. I raise doubts about the argument that early *yangwu* officials supported "feudal" parcelization and the old system itself.

Finally, Sasaki examines the formation of the "Disciplined Forces," a military reform carried out by Beijing during the Tongzhi Restoration. He argues that the Disciplined Forces had to depend on the authority of Han governors-general, and as a result, they played an auxiliary role to the volunteer troops.

In his essay "An Evaluation of Prewar Japanese Studies of the Early Westernization Movement"[a] (in *Sōritsu gojū shūnen kinen ronbunshū* [Collection of Essays Commemorating the 50th Anniversary]), Tajiri Toshi examines work by prewar Japanese scholars on the *yangwu* movement in China. In addition we have an another essay by Takahashi Kōsuke, "Encouraging Enterprise along the 'Route of the Itinerant Merchant': On Reading Mr. Xia Dongyuan's *Zheng Guanying zhuan* (A Biography of Zheng Guanying)"[c] (*Chikaki ni arite* 6). This work uses the ideas of Xia Dongyuan to introduce revisionist historiography in China.

Three other articles in this area are: Satō Shin'ichi, "On Zheng Guanying (Part 2): 'International Law' and 'Commercial War'"[b] (*Hōgaku* 48.4); Suzuki Tomoo, "The Unequal Treaties and the Early Westernization Group"[a] (in *Tanaka*); and Suzuki Tomoo, "The Distinctive Management Character of the Early Silk Industry in Guangdong as Seen from the 'Advertisements' in the *Tsun-wan yat-po*"[b] (*Chikaki ni arite* 6).

Satō addresses the thought and actions of Zheng Guanying, a man of comprador origins. He argues that Cheng was ever vigilant about the foreign powers' advances into China and farsightedly participated in the establishment and management of native industries. His ultimate objective, Satō claims, was neither "self-strengthening" nor the maintenance of the traditional system but to make China a participant in the international social order. In addition, Satō offers an analysis of the changes in Zheng's actions and ideas at the time of the Sino-French War. Scholars who give a positive assessment of the early Westernizers have often emphasized their national aims in confronting the Western powers; others have stressed essentially negative features. Satō's analysis gets to the root of the policies upon which these earlier evaluations have been based.

Both of Suzuki's articles offer a negative analysis of the *yangwu* group. The first argues that while one can recognize in the diplomatic policies of this group a certain trace of "resistance" and an orientation toward "treaty revisions," their ultimate aim was the preservation of the old system. One does not see the appearance of a "national defense consciousness" in the modern sense of the expression. His second essay uses fresh historical materials from the *Tsun-wan yat-po* and other sources. He argues that the early national capitalist silk industry in Guangdong was founded and supported through the authority of the local gentry (*shenshi* and *qilao*). Furthermore, the Qing officialdom, which included the early Westernizers at the time, never once offered protection or assistance to these national capitalists.

Among studies of foreign relations, Sasaki Masaya's essay, "A Study of the Opium War: From Pottinger's Arrival at His Post to the Conclusion of the Treaty of Nanjing (Part 2)"[a] (*Kindai Chūgoku* 15), discusses the arrival of Pottinger as well as the deceptiveness in the memorials of Yishan from a slightly earlier period. More parts of this essay will follow.

In "On the Anti-Foreign Incident in Shanghai in 1859" (*Tōyō shi kenkyū* 43.3),[a] Kani Hiroaki takes as his subject the attack on foreigners by Shanghai commoners sympathic to those personally harmed by the forced labor system (coolies) overseas. He argues that, although other diplomatic issues existed, the severity of this incident indicates that the Chinese authorities could have stopped the trade by an outright ban. Kani has also written "The Chinese Sealing of the Borders, as Seen from the Perspective of *juhua*[1] in the Late Qing"[b] (*Shichō* N.S. 15), in which he discusses sexual discrimination among overseas emigrants. From the 1860's women who were prevented from emigrating individually moved overseas through Hong Kong as *juhua*. At the same time, this restraint on women emigrating overseas was used as an excuse for not offering them protection.

Takahashi Akira's article, "The Second Open Door Notes of John Hay"[a] (*Jimbun kenkyū [ōsaka shiritsu daigaku bungakubu kiyō]* 35.5), examines the second open door notes of the United States and emphasizes the relationship between the structure of the "southeast mutual guarantee" and domestic conditions in the United States.

In addition, Nakamura Tadashi's essay "On the 'First Meeting of the British Commercial Associations in China'"[a] (in *Tanaka*) describes this gathering of representatives of the English meeting halls from various places in China that took place in Shanghai in 1919.

We can divide studies of popular rebellions between those concerning the Taiping Rebellion and those connected to the Boxer Uprising. Two essays involving the former are: Fukuda Setsuo and Tsutsumi Kazuyoshi, "One Trend in Sailors' Associations in Shandong and North of the Yangzi in the Late Qing: On the Activities of *fufei*"[a] (*Fukuoka joshi tandai kiyō* 27); and Nakada Yoshinobu, "The Evaluation of Du Wenxiu in China"[a] (*Kindai Chūgoku* 15).

The first of these essays argues that it may not necessarily be correct to see the *fufei* or *fu* bandits as a movement led by the local gentry. Rather the authors see the group as acting on the basis of horizontal bonds of cooperation and mutual aid. The essay by Nakada points out that Chinese evaluations of Du Wenxiu, a Muslim leader in the Dali regime in mid-19th century Yunnan, center on whether or not he had aligned with England. Nakada argues that Du's aims lay more in the self-defense of the Muslim community than in the overthrow of the Qing dynasty, and he doubts one can sustain an assessment of Du on the basis of whether he received foreign aid. As a critique of the "evaluative historical view," Nakada's analytic perspective is very suggestive.

Okuzaki Yūji's article, "The Lifestyle of the People as Seen in Morality Books of the Late Qing, from the Opium War through the Taiping Rebellion"[c] (in *Tanaka*), collects and comments on excerpts from morality books that demonstrate how the people lived in the period covered.

In his piece, "Studies of Taiping History in Modern China"[a] (*Kindai Chūgoku kenkyū ihō* 6), Kawabata Genji reexamines and comments on various themes in Chinese research on the Taipings. He also looks at the Chinese collections of historical materials and guides to them, published since 1979, such as the *Taiping tianguo guanxi lunwen mulu biao* (A List of Writings on Taiping Rebellion).

We should also note two other essays: Usui Yasuko, "Lai Wenguang, from the Taiping to the Nian Rebellion"[a] (*Eikyoshū* 1); and the second part of Kojima Shinji's translation (with commentary) of A. F. Lindley's book, *The Taeping as they are, by one of them*[a] [London, 1864] (*Rōhyakushō no sekai* 2).

A number of essays were concerned with the Boxer Uprising: Tessan Hiroshi, "Semi-Colonization in Late Qing Sichuan and the Anti-Christian Movement"[a] (*Rekishigaku kenkyū* 529); Tessan Hiroshi, "A Study of the 1891 Rebellion in Rehe and Chaoyang"[b] (*Chūgoku shi kenkyū* 8); and Satō Kimihiko, "The Jintandao Rebellion in Rehe in 1891"[b] (*Tōyō shi kenkyū* 43.2).

Tessan's first essay looks at anti-Christian struggles. Earlier theories have differentiated between comprador official-gentry and anti-religious official-gentry and have seen the "people" joining forces with the latter to continue the struggle. Tessan argues that, at least in the case of the Dazu anti-Christian fighting, the leadership of the Gelaohui emerged during the second period of the struggle, as people abandoned the conservative official-gentry and developed their own movement. He claims that they greatly influenced the Boxer movement.

His second essay and Satō's deal with the same 1891 uprising. Although this rebellion occurred early (according to Tessan), and was principally comprised of White Lotus sectarians (according to Satō), the rebels did crudely tie together the two issues of anti-imperialism and anti-feudalism (Tessan) and fought against them in their own cause (Satō).

Going back a bit in history to look at the relationship between religious organizations and anti-bureaucratic organizations, Noguchi Tetsurō has written "*Zhaifei* and *huifei*"[b] (in *Tanaka*). His point is that, since these two groups had the same roots, they came together. In the period from the Daoguang to the Tongzhi reigns, they shifted from *zhaifei* to *huifei*.

Many studies of the Boxers have classified the movement as one in a long line of "great anti-imperialist, anti-feudal movements of the people." In opposition to this approach, Mitsuishi Zenkichi ("The Boxers and the Origin of 'Using the People to Control the Barbarians'",[a] in *Tanaka*) sees the Boxers from the point of view of the Chinese imperial state. He argues that essentially the Boxer Uprising was the climax of the anti-Christian movement led by the gentry from 1860 on. However, he sees that, on the one hand, secret societies raised the banner of the dawning of a Utopian, new age and, on the other, radicalized the gentry's strategy of "using the people to control the barbarians." These converged in a "cultural, racial, millenialist movement" (that is, an "early nationalism"), which secularized the main leadership of the conservative, orthodox group. The limitations of the Boxers' "anti-imperialism and anti-feudalism" are based in this "cultural, racial millenialism."

In the field of Sino-Japanese relations, we have an essay on how the Japanese learned of the Opium War and Taiping Rebellion and what influence they exercised in Japan: Haga Noboru, "The Opium War, the Taiping Rebellion, and Japan"[a] (in *Tanaka*). Sasaki Yō's article, "Views of Japan Held by Qing Officials in the Tongzhi Reign: The Period Culminating in the Conclusion of the Articles of Sino-Japanese Friendship"[a] (*Saga daigaku kyōiku gakubu kenkyū ronbunshū* 31.2), discusses Qing official knowledge of Japan, primarily of Japanese efforts to introduce Western technology. Kojima Shinji's essay, "Japan during the Meiji Period, as Seen from China"[a] (*Rekishi kōron* 10.3), looks mainly at how Chinese views of Japan shifted after the high-tide of Chinese study in Japan. In "Notes on the Chinese Translation of *Meiji ishin shi* [History of the Meiji Restoration]"[b] (*Shingai kakumei kenkyū* 4), Nakamura Tadashi looks at the publication of a Chinese translation of a work on the Meiji Restoration to examine images of Japan held by Chinese readers.

Iwakabe Yoshimitsu's article, "The Sino-Japanese War and the Problem of Chinese Residents in Japan: 'Imperial Edict No. 137' of 1894 and the Residential Area in Yokohama"[a] (*Hōsei shigaku* 36), discusses both the forms and reality of how resident Chinese in Japan were treated during the period of the Sino-Japanese War of 1894-95. In "Sending Chinese Students to Japan in the Early Period, Primarily the Period of the 1898 Reform Movement"[a] (*Shingai kakumei kenkyū* 4), Kobayashi Tomoaki examines the policy adopted to send Chinese overseas to study in Japan after the Sino-Japanese War, and the policies of China and Japan themselves, from the perspective of international relations. There is also Horiguchi Isamu's "Negotiations Leading to the Conclusion of the 'Sino-Japanese Treaty on Sea Trade'"[a] (*Chūō shigaku* 7).

Suzuki Ken'ichi's article, "The Technical Academy of Port Arthur"[a] (in *Tanaka*), discusses the academy as part of Japan's program of advancement into Manchuria. In addition, we have volumes by Satō Saburō, *Kindai Nit-Chū kōshō shi no kenkyū* (A Study of the History of Modern Sino-Japanese Relations)[a]; and Nishimura Shigeo, *Chūgoku kindai Tōhoku chiiki shi kenkyū* (A Study of the History of the Northeastern Region in Modern China),[a] which examines Northeast China, centering on the "Japanese colonial empire." Both of these books deserve reviews.

The development of indigenous industry has thus far been most successfully treated by scholars in the field of light industry, while the area of heavy industry has not been as thoroughly handled. For this reason, Shima Ichirō's essay, "The Development of the Domestic Machine Industry in Modern China: Its History and Structure of Production"[a] (*Keizaigaku ronsō* 33.2-4), is very valuable. He argues that the importance of the machine industry, as the industry that produced the means of production [for other industries—JAF], lay in its close connection with both light industry and agriculture. For the purpose of distinguishing kinds of industry, he divides the history of the Shanghai machine industry into four stages. He then focuses attention on the first half of the 1930's, and through an analysis of the structure of production he points out the industry's character and limitations, particularly in Shanghai.

We also have an essay by Sōda Saburō that analyzes the growth of the mechanized silk industry in Shanghai in relation to world markets: "Shanghai Mechanized Silk on World Silk Markets"[a] (*Shigaku kenkyū* 163). Sōda argues that Shanghai mechanically-produced silk was of a high quality, with strong links to the market in Lyon, but that it could not compete with cheaper Japanese silk, a product of uniform quality, linked with the American market. However, the decline in French imports, beginning in the early 20th century, and the decline in European silk supplies for the American market during World War I spurred the advance of Chinese silk into American markets.

Ōno Santoku's article, "The Nature and Development of Rong Family Enterprises Prior to the 1911 Revolution"[a] (*Kōchi kōgyō kōtō senmon gakkō gakujutsu kiyō* 20), analyzes the enterprises of the Rong family, native bankers and cocoon wholesalers who went into business at the time of the Boxer Uprising.

I would like next to look at research on the 1898 Reform Movement and the 1911 Revolution. Fujitani Kōetsu's essay, "Problems in the Study of the 1898 Reform Movement"[a] (*Shingai kakumei kenkyū* 4), discusses recent trends in research. He suggests that we need to analyze the behavior of the leaders in this period. We should consider the reasons for their failure and distinguish between their subjective motives and the objective results of their actions. We also have a piece by Fukazawa Hideo, "The 1898 Reform Movement and the Zhiyong Academy in Liuyang County, Hunan"[b] (*Arutesu riberaresu* 34).

On the revolutionary movement, Kojima Yoshio's "On the Chinese National Assembly (Part 3)"[a] (*Shingai kakumei kenkyū* 4) deals with the activities of the Chinese National Assembly in Fujian and Shandong.

In addition, we have two essays by Matsumoto Takehiko: "The Founding and Character of the 'United Association of Overseas Chinese of the Republic of China'"[b] (in *Tanaka*); and "The Dare-to-Die Corps of Overseas Chinese in Japan at the Time of the 1911 Revolution"[c] (in *Okamoto*). Both pieces look at the response of overseas Chinese to the 1911 Revolution. The former treats the "United Association of Overseas Chinese of the Republic of China" which was organized in and around Kōbe, and analyzes the background of the groups supporting the revolution.

In "Henry George's Thought and Its Reception in Japan and China: The Land Policies of Sun Yat-sen, Miyazaki Tamizō, and Abe Isoo"[a] (*Shirin* 67.5), Ihara Takushū looks at the differences between the Chinese and Japanese reception of Henry George's notion of a Single Tax.

Nozawa Yutaka, in his article "Zhang Jian and the Economic Policies of the Yuan Shikai Regime in the Early Republican Period"[b] (*Chikaki ni arite* 5), reexamines the policies of the Beijing government, which have thus far been seen as playing an obstructive role in the development of Chinese capitalism. He focuses on the programs of Zhang Jian, head of the Bureau of Agriculture under Yuan, and he points out that the structure of commercial law, aimed at the encouragement of business, began to take shape during Zhang Jian's term of office.

Hamashita Takeshi's essay, "China's Monetary Reform and Foreign Banks"[c] (*Gendai Chūgoku* 58), summarizes his work on the monetary reforms that began in 1898. Fujii Shōzō's essay, "On Materials Concerning the 1911 Revolution Compiled by the Old [Japanese] Admiralty"[a] (*Shingai kakumei kenkyū* 4), introduces documentary materials involving the Revolution of 1911 from the old admiralty, held in the Defense Training Institute of the Japanese Defense Agency.

I would like now to turn to work on the thought and behavior of modern Chinese reformers. First, on Kang Youwei we have an essay by Nakamura Satoru, "Kang Youwei's Understanding of the Classics: On the Relationship between Classical Scholarship and the Reception of Western Learning"[a] (*Tōyō daigaku daigakuin kiyō* 20). He doubts that all of Kang's basic ideas derive directly from the theory of the Three Ages (*sanshi*) which comes from the *Gongyang Commentary* on the *Spring and Autumn Annals*. Kang's reformist thought, Nakamura argues, originated in Western learning. We also have two essays by Beppu Sunao: "Kang Youwei's Scholarship and Xunzi (Part 1)"[a] (*Tetsugaku shisō ronshū* 9); and "The West and Tradition in Liang Qichao"[b] (*Rinrigaku* 2).

Tang Zhijun's essay (trans. Kondō Kuniyasu), "The 1911 Revolution and Zhang Binglin"[a] (*Shisō* 725), discusses how classical studies changed and what role they played in the ideas of Chinese revolutionaries of the late Qing. He examines the relationship between Zhang Binglin and Confucian scholarship as well as the role Zhang played in the 1911 Revolution. He also concisely sums up the earlier conflicting views of Kang Youwei and Zhang Binglin on reform vs. revolution and the Chinese classics (new vs. old text traditions).

In the same issue of *Shisō*, there is Kondō Kuniyasu's article, "The Post-1949 Generation in China and Studies in Intellectual History: Tang Zhijun and Li Zehou."[a] Through an examination of the writings on Kang Youwei and Zhang Binglin by Tang and Li, Kondō sees Li's analysis as essentially between the West (symbolized by liberty, equality, philanthropy) and China (the consciousness of small peasant producers), while Tang poses a break between the contemporary period (socialist China) and antiquity (classical scholarship). He sees the problematic of research on modern Chinese intellectual history to be considerably different in China and Japan, but the relationship between them, he argues, remains complementary.

Two other works concerning Zhang Binglin should be noted, both by Takata Atsushi: "Wang Chuanshan in the Late Qing"[a] (*Gakushūin daigaku bungakubu kenkyū nempō* 30); and *Shingai kakumei to Shō Heirin no seibutsu tetsugaku* (The 1911 Revolution and Zhang Binglin's Philosophy of the Equality of All Things).[b] The first piece examines the image of Wang Chuanshan [Wang Fuzhi, 1619-1692] projected by the revolutionaries of the late Qing. Many late Qing thinkers distanced themselves from Wang's racialism and even criticized him, but one who continued to maintain this line of thought until after the revolution was Zhang Binglin. What Wang represented to Zhang, according to Takata, was the "notion of an ethnic culture" linked to race. Takata's book examines Zhang's "philosophy of the equality of all things," which he sees as an intellectual manifestation of Zhang's political activities from 1898 forward, as well as one result of Sino-Western scholarly thought in the late Qing and early 20th century. This volume should be reviewed all by itself.

Arita Kazuo's book, *Shinmatsu ishiki kōzō no kenkyū* (A Study of the Structure of Late Qing Consciousness),[a] examines the "consciousness" of individual human beings and takes the overall trends that unify these individuals to be a "consciousness situation." He posits the mechanism of a "structure of consciousness," as thought emerges from the mutual influence of these two forces: individuals and the overall trends. He then uses this notion of a structure of consciousness to investigate various ideas of the late Qing. Takata Atsushi has written a book review which appears in *Chūgoku kenkyū geppō* (437).

In "Tang Caichang's Idea of *tong*"[a] (*Chūtetsu bungaku kaihō* 9), Fujii Tomoko argues that Tang's notion of *tong* as a consciousness of politics and the world was based on a Sino-foreign concept rooted in "civilization," did not include "anti-foreign" or "anti-Manchu" political ideas, was patterned on "public law," and was a general principle of "great harmony" that was to be realized through the illumination of men's intellectual powers.

Nishizato Yoshiyuki's essay, "Wang Tao and the *Tsun-wan yat-po*"[a] (*Tōyō shi kenkyū* 43.3), outlines Wang's career as a person who always cooperated with two opposing forces and, while groping for a personal stand as a point of contact, continuously looked for a way toward a Chinese national revival. He also examines the newspaper Wang founded, *Tsun-wan yat-po*.

Fukazawa Hideo, in "The Modernization of China and Yung Wing"[c] (in *Tanaka*), describes the relationship between Yung Wing and a variety of forces. Shinozaki Moritoshi, in his "Yang Dusheng in the Period of the Hunan Reform Movement"[a] (*Kumatsu shū* 4), traces Yang's career and his thought before going to Japan. Ikezawa Miyoshi, in his "Jiang Zhiyou's Satire, from 'Nucai hao' ["The Slave is Fine," the name of a poem by Jiang—JAF] to the Zhengwen Association"[a] (*Bunka* 48.1-2), examines Cai Zhiyou's thought and his lifestyle through his vernacular poetry.

In his essay "On the Conception of a Republic of Five Ethnicities in the Period of the 1911 Revolution"[a] (in *Tanaka*), Kataoka Kazutada argues against the "accepted theory" that Sun Zhongshan (Sun Yat-sen) was the originator of the "conception of a republic of five ethnic groups." He claims that Sun's nationalism was a racial assimilationist conception that originated in the great nationalism of Liang Qichao and in the views of Wang Jingwei who criticized Liang.

Tomita Noboru has written "The Formation of Li Dazhao's Thought during His Period of Study in Japan: On the Emergence of the Concept of *minyi*"[b] (*Shūkan Tōyōgaku* 51). He looks at Li's reception of Marxism and examines principally the formation of Li's basic notion of *minyi* [populism or "rule of the people"—JAF].

Ōsato Hiroaki's piece, "A Draft Chronological Biography of Tao Chengzhang (Part 1)"[a] (*Rōhyakushō no sekai* 2), adopts the technique of the chronological biography, and through the author's detective work fills in gaps in the historical materials. It is fascinating.[2]

Concerning the history of Taiwan, we should note that during the past year two journals ran issues devoted to Taiwan: "Special Issue: An Enthusiastic Look from Okinawa to Taiwan" (*Shin Okinawa bungaku* 60); and "Special Issue: Japan's Postwar Responsibility and Asia" (*Kikan san-*

zenri 41). The encounter between Okinawa and Taiwan in the modern period was an unhappy meeting—the dispatching of troops to Taiwan in 1874 was based on the pretext of the sufferings of Okinawans in Taiwan and diplomatic negotiations at the time of the sending of troops to Taiwan launched the Meiji government in its determined actions against the Ryūkyū Islands.

Matakichi Morikiyo's "Control over the Colony of Taiwan and Okinawa(ns)"[a] (*Shin Okinawa bungaku* 60) shows how the Okinawa Incident was cunningly used in colonial education on Taiwan and the place given to Okinawans in the hierarchical structure of colonial society. He also touches on the complex relationship between Okinawa and Taiwan under Japanese imperialism.

The discussion between Dai Guohui and Kang Jae-on in this issue of *Kikan sanzenri* is fascinating. Starting from the issue of "why we must examine the relationship between Japan and Asia as based in Taiwan," their discussion diverges into such areas as the land survey projects and the monopoly systems in Taiwan and Korea that were organized in a highly complex manner under Japanese colonial rule. In the past the confluence of Korean and Okinawan historical studies were seen as issues for the development of studies of Taiwan's history itself, and this past year a first step has been taken in this direction.

The journal *Taiwan kin-gendai shi kenkyū* (5) devoted an issue to the Qing period in Taiwan. Christian Daniels' essay, "The Structure of the Sugar Industry in Southern Taiwan during the Qing Dynasty, Especially Prior to 1860,"[b] looks at the development of the Taiwanese sugar industry, including its fusion with mainland markets, landlord-tenant relations in the cultivation of sugar cane and sugar production, and the emergence of a sugar industry commonly managed by the direct producers. He presents the first overall view of the sugar industry in the Qing dynasty. On the stages of development of this industry prior to the Japanese occupation of Taiwan, Dai Guohui claimed some years ago that by the early 18th century the industry "had reached a stage on the verge of manufacture" (in *Chūgoku kanshōtōgyō no tenkai* [The Development of the Chinese Sugar Cane Industry].[a] While Daniels agrees with Dai that there were specialized and cooperative modes of production, he maintains against Dai that the sugar workers were not simple wage laborers, but seasonal workers who "always returned to being peasants."

Hayashi Masako's essay in the same issue, "Xi Zufan and Regulations for the Training of Troops throughout Taiwan: A Reinvestigation of Materials Concerning Taiwan in the Late Qing,"[a] examines Liu Ao, Inspector General of Taiwan, who hid in the shadows of Liu Mingchuan, the early Governor of

Taiwan. She reassesses the view that Liu Mingchuan was an "enlightened politician." She also discusses the formation of an ethnic consciousness in late Qing Taiwan through a study of the armed struggles against the Japanese occupation until the period of World War I. These also have been described by Wakabayashi Masafumi, in his book *Taiwan kō-Nichi undō shi kenkyū* (A Study of the History of the Anti-Japanese Movement in Taiwan),[b] as "strongly resembling the 'anti-official mobs' of the Qing era."

In their article, "Han Chinese Immigrants and Ethnicity: The Cases of Hong Kong and Taiwan"[a] (*Minzokugaku kenkyū* 84.4), Wang Songxing and Segawa Masahisa discuss Taiwan in the late Qing (from 1860 on) as "changing from an immigrant society to a native society." As for the rise of ethnic consciousness in Hong Kong, with the intrusion of the British Army during the Opium War, they should have addressed the many-faceted historical links between anti-British protest and clan feuds and popular uprisings.

Also concerning Taiwan in the Qing is Ishibashi Takao's "An Annotated Translation of the Secret Memorials of Gioroi Mamboo Concerning Taiwan in the *Gongzhong dang'an Kangxi chao zouzhe*"[b] (*Chūgoku kindai shi kenkyū* 4). He has translated the reports from 1712 to 1722 written by the Manchu bannerman Mamboo who was serving as Governor of Fujian and Governor-General of Fujian and Zhejiang. It is a painstaking work useful for research on the early period of the Qing occupation of Taiwan in that, for example, through it we learn of rice prices in Fujian and Taiwan.

Liu Jinqing's essay "An Examination of the Character of Landownership in Traditional Taiwanese Society"[a] (*Tōkyō keidai gakkai shi* 37) follows generally accepted theories of land management in late Qing Taiwan, which are based on Okamatsu Santarō's works: *Taiwan shihō* (Private Law in Taiwan)[a] and *Taiwan shūkan kiji* (Articles on Taiwanese Customs).[b] He explains that "real power over agricultural land actually moved into the hands of small tenant households."

My article, "Rural Merchants and the Export of Grain in Taiwan during the Qing"[b] (*Taiwan kin-gendai shi kenkyū* 5), asks whether we need a cautious reexamination of past arguments that rural merchants with commercial capital participated in the management of water control systems.

On Okamatsu Santarō and the research [project carried out under his guidance] concerning the old customs [of Taiwan], Haruyama Meitetsu ("The Investigation of Taiwanese Customs and the Question of Legislation,"[a] *Shin Okinawa bungaku* 60), observes the lack of integration between the six-three educational law and the Meiji Constitution. He has also written "The 'Old Customs' and the 'Law' in a Colony"[b] (*Kikan sanzenri* 41).

Nakamura Fujie's piece, "The Tombstone Inscription of Pihowaris: Remembering Mr. Gao Yongqing"[a] (*Taiwan kin-gendai shi kenkyū* 5), concerns

Gao Yongqing, who was a living witness to the Wushe Incident. There is also Wakamori Tamio's "Introducing a Source, Gao Yongqing's Memoirs: The Wushe Incident and Studies of It"[a] (*Tōhō gakuen daigaku tanki daigakubu kiyō* 3). Mr. Gao's notes were entrusted to Nakamura, and it is hoped that this historical description of a man who was suppressed at the time will be made public.

Finally, I would like to take note of the three-volume work *Taiwan gendai shōsetsu sen* (Selections from Contemporary Taiwanese Novels),[a] (ed. Matsunaga Masayoshi and others, with commentaries by Matsunaga and Wakabayashi Masafumi); and Chen Zhengti's essay, " 'Chinese Consciousness' and 'Taiwanese Consciousness' in Taiwan: On Recent Debates in Literary and Intellectual Circles"[a] (*Chūgoku kenkyū geppō* 439).

5

Ming-Qing Studies in Japan: 1985

Norimatsu Akifumi, in *Shigaku zasshi*
95.5 (May 1986), 214-221.

As we move into the latter half of the 1980's, postwar historical research on the Ming and Qing periods continues along well-trodden paths. From last year's eighty or more books and articles in this field, it is difficult to discern either works introducing fresh perspectives or those representing distinctive orientations. We have not yet fully broken away from our present state of confusion, perhaps even stagnation. However, one can point to three symposia as examples of directions being taken in today's research: "Problems Concerning Rent Resistance Struggles,"[a] Hokkaidō University, 1980; "The Perspective of Local Society: Local Society and Leadership,"[a] Nagoya University, 1981; and "A Reinvestigation of State 'Control' and the Image of the People in Yuan, Ming, and Qing Times,"[a] Kyūshū University, 1983. These three have borne considerable fruit, but because the themes raised were quite distinct, we have not reached the point where they can offer mutual criticism and shared perspectives for analysis. Nonetheless, we may still note the following directions.

Ming-Qing historical research in the 1960's and 1970's centered around "theories of the gentry" (*kyōshin ron*). These theories emerged from work on the historical development of taxation and labor service systems. They were shaped by an acute awareness of the power structure of autocratic state authority in China; and through an analysis of the state-established *institutions* of land tax and labor service, they sought to elucidate the distinctive Chinese social structure of the period. In this process, though, production relations—as represented in landlord-tenant relations—together with the structure of production and productive capacity, became central concerns. Scholars either undervalued or neglected problems of commerce, commodity circulation, markets, and transportation. They ignored the existence of urban dwellers, bullies, and vagrants who cannot be understood solely from the perspective of landlord-tenant relations. They paid little attention to the nature of a distinctive Chinese ethnic cohesion in clans and lineages which formed basic human communities, as well as to religious ceremonies and beliefs. In fact, it is by elucidating these distinctive Chinese social patterns of the Ming and Qing periods that we may see production relations, the structure of production, and productive capacity in the context of human relations. This is the way to attempt an understanding of Ming-Qing social structure.

Let us look first at the landlord system. Miki Satoshi's essay "The Development of Rent Resistance in Fujian in the Qing"[a] (*Hokkaidō daigaku bungakubu kiyō* 34.1) basically follows previous views of rent resistance from the late Ming on. According to these views, the historical development of the direct producers or small peasantry finds concentrated expression in the contradictions of landlord-tenant relations. Miki first examines model cases of rent resistance in Fujian over the nearly 250 years between the Wanli and the Daoguang reigns; he subdivides them into four periods for convenience; and he recognizes a "continuous," "geographic, spatial" development.

Miki next analyzes in detail local customs described in the Qianlong edition of the *Chongan xian zhi* (Gazetteer of Chongan County), held in the Fujian Provincial Library. He argues three basic points. First, although rent resistance was carried out within the framework of the then standard one-field two-owners system, landlords responded to this dual ownership system with basic tolerance and prescribed control. Second, the "*tuhao*," or local bullies as the term appears in historical sources, were men involved with tenant farmers as lenders of silver or grain (Miki assumes these were locally resident usurer capitalists and merchant capitalists—namely rice merchants). However, conflict emerged between landlords and local bullies because the repayment of these loans was made in grain at the time of rent payment [in silver]. In response tenant farmers favored the bullies and practiced rent resistance against the landlords. The fact was that "loans from *tuhao*, for production capital in agricultural management or for rice in lean periods between harvests," were essential to a tenant farmer's survival and the reproduction of his means of production. Third, state power in the early Qing controlled rent resistance through direct intervention and a unified *baojia* system.

We can point to two essays which enable us to see where studies of rent resistance are headed at present: the written report on the Hokkaidō University symposium (in *Shihō* 15 [1982]) and Mori Masao's summary of the history of research (in *Kōso to nuhen* [Rent Resistance and Bondservant Uprisings]).[b] These pieces both raise numerous issues, but especially the importance of placing rent resistance within the context of popular struggles, and of understanding various kinds of struggles—tax resistance, grain theft, bondservant uprisings, and religious rebellions—from a unified perspective. I will touch on this point below. What is needed is not that our attention be drawn to the phenomenon of "rent resistance" itself, but that we analyze rent resistance, linking the social circumstances of both landlord and tenant (including commerce, circulation of goods, markets, and human relations, as mentioned above), with social upheavals. On the basis of such an analysis one can then reassess the historical significance of rent resistance.

Miki's references to the structure of markets and commodity circulation may be valuable as a step in this direction. Let me now examine several points with respect to his essay. First, he only recognizes the "development of rent resistance" temporally, geographically, and spatially, and hence does not offer an explanation of its qualitative growth or of its periodization. Second, an analysis of the organization and territorial cohesion of tenant farmers, who were the main actors in rent resistance, is absolutely essential. Third, although this analysis, in conjunction with the concrete historical sources, is worthy of our attention, even if we accept that "*tuhao*" had some point of contact with merchants out of a need to circulate the grain that accumulated as debt repayment, there is no objective basis for regarding them as "local rice merchants." Also, Miki points to the possibility of a " 'wholesale advance payment' form of production," but this concept remains extremely vague. Fourth, Miki agrees that tenant farmers in South and Central China in the Ming and Qing periods, as earlier, understood rice as a necessity for maintaining the reproduction of their means of production, but can we now see this condition as universal for China? If this were the case, then we would have to investigate within the structure of reproduction such questions as the amount of rice which tenant farmers used for their own food and its ratio to other foodstuffs (wheat, soy beans, and potatoes), and whether they grew it or obtained it by other means, as well as its kinds, qualities, and value.

Kawakatsu Mamoru has written an article entitled "One Source on Landlord Management in Jiangnan in the First Half of the 19th Century"[c] (*Tōyō shi ronshū* 14). Its subtitle—"Through an Analysis of *Jiaqing zubu*, Held in the Kyūshū University Library"—indicates that he analyzes these particular landlord account books from the Jiaqing era, and he does so in great detail, using charts and diagrams. Through them he tries to clarify aspects of landlord management in the 19th century. He notes, for example, that although farm rent was principally paid in grain, rent could be paid in cash, or even for certain tenants in beans; that it was possible for summer wheat to play the supplementary role of autumn rent; and that a tenant's familial relations were useful to a landlord for the stability of his operations.

Kawakatsu's conclusions combine this research with work he is doing on the rent account books held in the library of the Research Institute for Humanistic Sciences at Kyoto University. Let me mention just two of his conclusions. First, he notes that farm rent was set on the basis of the individual relationship between a landlord and a tenant. Previously, we tended to argue that farm rent was uniformly fixed by the landlord for all the tenants under him. Kawakatsu's argument suggests we need further elucidation of the mechanisms for fixing rents. His second point is that rent arrears going back to the Qianlong period were treated as rent arrears in the *Jiaqing zubu* and that there are cases of their settlement clearly noted in the account books with specific yearly amounts from Qianlong times. He cites instances from these account books in which the amount of rent arrears was not settled and asks whether there was a statute of limitations on the liquidation of arrears. Kawakatsu sharply alters our previous understanding of rent resistance, and we await further work on his part.

As noted earlier, in recent years attention has returned to the distinctive ethnic cohesion of Chinese society, such as in the clan or local lineage. In addition to the essays by Miki and Kawakatsu which touch on this issue, we have a valuable piece by Mori Masao, "The *Hsiang-tsu*"[c] (*Tōyō shi kenkyū* 44.1), which introduces the theories of Fu Yiling, Yang Guozhen, and Sen Ge. Also, there is Tanaka Issei's volume, *Chūgoku no sōzoku to engeki* (Clan and Drama in China).[a]

Other works in this general field include two pieces on the one-field two-owners system: Terada Hiroaki, "On *Chengjia, guotou*, and *dingshou*, as Seen in the *Chongming xian zhi*"[b] (*Tōyō bunka kenkyūjo kiyō* 98); and Fujii Hiroshi, "A New Study of the Early One-Field Two-Owners System"[b] (*Tōhōgaku* 69). Also, Kusano Yasushi's volume, *Chūgoku no jinushi keizai* (China's Landlord Economy),[a] was recently published and has already elicited a review by Matsuda Yoshirō in *Tōyō shi kenkyū* (44.3).

Research into the history of popular uprisings and religious rebellions has been booming. Unlike studies of rent resistance, however, work in this area has been keenly attentive to its place in the general history of popular uprisings. Recent research has offered serious analyses of *Baoquan*, the sacred scriptures of popular religion, and last year a number of comprehensive studies were published by scholars who have been considering these topics for many years. Kobayashi Kazumi's essay, "Religious Rebellions in the Qing Dynasty"[b] (in *Chūsei*) is a magnificent piece which addresses the historical significance of religious uprisings—White Lotus, Taipings, and Boxers—at the same time taking account of both rent resistance and tax resistance.

Kobayashi's theory is extremely suggestive, and I would like to make special mention of one of his hypotheses. He argues that economic struggles—such as rent and tax resistance—had a distinctive place in the history of reform insofar as they brought about an understanding of reform as "social revolution (land revolution)." This could give rise to a transformation of the economic base, as opposed to change within the superstructure, as in a "political revolution." In cases of the latter, the religious rebellions of the Qing period realized a "communistic communitarian kingdom" that was subject to discrimination and oppression by the establishment. Kobayashi's essay provides a clear explanation of well-known views he suggested in 1973.

In "Associations of 'Heterodox Teachings' and the Populace in the Ming and Qing"[c] (*Shichō* N. S. 18), Noguchi Tetsurō discusses his overall views, and Asai Motoi offers an appended summary and criticism. Noguchi examines the relationship between "heterodox religious" groups and the populace from the perspective of their this-worldly ambitions, and he sees late Ming changes in religious groups as something born of convenience in the interests of secular goals. Asai's critique emphasizes the fusion that took place between the Luo and White Lotus Sects. He also notes that these changes may simply have been based on the nature of these groups' religious beliefs. I should also like to mention the publication of Noguchi's book, *Mindai Byakurenkyō shi no kenkyū* (Studies in the History of the White Lotus Sect in the Ming Period).[d]

Asai has also written "The Transmission of the Way in the Blue Lotus Sect of the Qing Dynasty"[b] (in *Nishi*). He argues that during the Qing period the religious influence of the Blue Lotus Sect grew and split the sect into smaller denominations.

Although each of these three scholars—Kobayashi, Noguchi, and Asai—evaluates religious uprisings as positive historical movements, Noguchi and Asai see the rebellions as one part of a mass millenarian movement. They try to understand these religious groups and their members by stressing their relationship to social and economic actualities of the time. By contrast, Kobayashi seeks to explain the history of popular thought and the internal world of the people through an analysis of popular religious beliefs, at the same time seeing these religious associations from a political perspective.

We should pay particular attention to the views of Kobayashi and Yasuno Shōzō, among others, concerning the necessity of closely examining the junctures at which people entered these religious societies, looking especially at the differences between Jiangnan and North China. In this connection, one should take a look at Asai Motoi's review (in *Tōyō shi kenkyū* 43.3 [1984]) of the volume *Zoku Chūgoku minshū hanran no sekai* (The World of Popular Rebellion in China, Continued),[a] ed. Seinen Chūgoku kenkyūsha kaigi (Conference of young China scholars). The report of the aforementined symposium at Kyūshū University and the article by Yasuno to be discussed below are also relevant here. In any event, the debate between the two positions outlined above is not over, nor have the disputants yet to face each other directly. One hopes that an exchange of critiques will advance scholarship in this area.

One further piece worth our attention is Ōsawa Akihiro's "An Investigation of Religious Rebellion in the Late Ming"[a] (*Tōyō shi kenkyū* 44.1). He examines the case of Qiao Jishi of Henan Province in the Wanli reign period and argues that the bond formed between [illegal—JAF] silver miners and local religious societies spelled the emergence of a religious rebellion of a new sort, shaped by the growth of a silver and commercial produce economy in the late Ming. He considers the late Ming an epochal period for religious uprisings. Although the relationship between religious rebellion and the social and economic background of the late Ming is, as Ōsawa generally argues, undeniable, we still need an analysis from this very perspective. I should also mention the publication last year of a book by Satō Fumitoshi, *Minmatsu nōmin hanran no kenkyū* (Studies of Peasant Rebellions of the Late Ming)[b]; book reviews are expected.

As I mentioned at the outset, one direction in recent research has been an interest in commerce, commodity circulation, markets, and the like. The "development of commercial products, their circulation, and a money economy," generally taken as the "formula" proving social and economic growth in the Ming and Qing, may, on reflection, not necessarily be all that apparent. At the same time, this growth is something considered to have positive significance.

Two essays examine the Huaian tax collection station located at a transportation hub for the Yangzi River, the Huai River, and the Grand Canal. They are: Kōsaka Masanori, "Commodity Circulation on the Grand Canal in the Qing Era"[b] (*Tōhoku gakuin daigaku ronshū* 15); and Takino Shōjirō, "On the Structure and Function of the Huaian Tax Collection Station in the Qing Era"[a] (*Tōyō shi ronshū* 14).

Kōsaka's article continues his recent work on the Xushu tax collection station during the Qing dynasty. Here, however, he gives an actual picture of commodity circulation along the Grand Canal in the Qianlong period, claiming that commodities moving South far surpassed those going North and that the primary commodities were soy bean products from Shandong and Henan.

Takino's essay discusses the function and personnel of the Huaian tax collection station. Whereas Kōsaka sees these stations as confiscatory, Takino is interested in the functional relationships between them and the surrounding localities. Thus, he argues, in the face of customs collections and unfair requisitions, merchants pioneered new transport routes and organizations to evade the stations. This led to the dispersal and expansion of commodity circulation and transport contacts via secondary transport routes to the Grand Canal, a development which enriched surrounding districts and had an adverse effect on the tax-collecting centers themselves.

Takino also clarifies his differences with Kōsaka over the Huaian station. He doubts the assertion that the volume of commodities going South exceeded that sent North, because Kōsaka's estimate is based only on those commodities that passed through customs stations. This point aside, we also have to look at the transport hubs along the Grand Canal as part of an overall grid of land and sea North-South commodity routes which did not pass through customs stations. Also, we need analyses of the economic structure of the areas near the stations by examining not just the quantity but also the kind of commodities involved. One essay that refers to the maritime transport of soy bean products from North to South China is Matsuura Akira's "Merchant Shipping and Coastal Transport in Jiangnan in the Qing Period"[a] (*Kansai daigaku bungaku ronshū* 34.3-4). One hopes that this notion of "secondary transport routes" raised in Takino's article will become conceptually clearer. We also need further explanation of when trade expansion into the region surrounding the Huaian station took place and of how this affected it.

I have written a piece entitled "Grain Circulation and Fluctuations in the Price of Rice in the Yongzheng Period"[a] (*Tōyō shi ronshū* 14). Using documents from the Palace Archives for the Yongzheng period, I see grain circulation and rice price fluctuations as interrelated. From this perspective I discuss the relationship between the circulation of grain and the pricing of rice in Suzhou Prefecture (Jiangsu) as well as in Quanzhou and Zhangzhou Prefectures (Fujian). In these districts, I argue, changes in the price of rice reflect structural changes regulated by the system of grain circulation over the wider area. I see this pattern of circulation and pricing as taking shape from the late Ming and early Qing on. We need now to look at concrete cases as well as to study the circulation-pricing pattern in the context of the structure of production and markets as well as that of merchant activity.

In his essay "Private Markets and the *shenshi* Gentry Stratum in Shantung in the Qing Period"[d] (*Tōyō gakuhō* 66.1-4), Yamane Yukio bases himself on previous work on North China markets to argue that *shiji*, rural tax-free markets, were controlled by the "resident lower gentry stratum"—namely, *shengyuan*, *gongsheng*, and *jiansheng*. He uses the case of the Xizou *shiji* in Qufu on the grounds of the local prefect's estate, and he examines the antagonistic relations between the local prefect, the lower gentry, and state power. One is still left without complete clarity about these relations or about the actual nature of the control exercised by the gentry as a group over the *shiji*.

Satō Manabu's article, "Shop Functionaries and Their Reform in Nanjing in the Ming Dynasty"[c] (*Kokushikan daigaku bungakubu jimbun gakkai kiyō* 17), argues that in the Ming period these shop functionaries procured goods for the state from commercial and industrial men in the cities. Seen from this perspective, *hang* in the Ming dynasty were "subordinate organizations" into which the state grouped commercial and industrial concerns according to type for the purposes of exacting labor service. He argues that there is little possibility that these correspond to *hang* as voluntary commoner unions of merchants in the same trade. Several dubious points remain. Can we, as Satō claims, see the work performed by these shop functionaries as "unilateral confiscation by the state?" What were these *hang* actually like?

In "Notes on Piaohao, Shanxi"[b] (*Shūkan Tōyōgaku* 54), Terada Takanobu introduces stories about Chinese from Piaohao based on materials found locally during a trip there. He argues that since there are hardly any records concerning Piaohao in the local gazetteer of Tianjin, its administrative center, we have to reexamine the historical accuracy of gazetteers themselves. One wonders if this point can be substantiated.

Studies of taxation and labor service systems and the structure of rural control, among the main themes of research in the 1960's and 1970's, have been numerous in recent years. Among these systems, the Community Elder or *lilaoren* office has been seen as one fostering state indoctrination in rural villages under the *lijia* system of the Ming dynasty. Wada Hironori ("The *lijia* System, the Lishe Altar, and the Xiangwan Altar,"[a] in *Nishi*) looks at the Lishe and Xiangwan altars which were set up by the Ming state in every village throughout the nation. He regards them as a means of spiritual control over the populace. The management of these two altars was the work of the *lizhang* and later the village elder or *changlao*. He argues that as the *lijia* system began to crumble after the mid-Ming, ceremonial institutions established under the coercive power of the *lijia* system declined; by contrast, popular White Lotus and Daoist sects flourished. Wada points out that the management of these two altars became a heavy burden for the *lizhang*, but they undergirded the power of the resident landlord stratum which supported the *lijia* system.

Yamamoto Eiji's essay, "An Explanation of the Poll Tax Levy in North China in the Early Qing"[a] (in *Nishi*), offers an analysis of the "Bianshen lun" by Huang Liu-hung. He argues that Huang was deeply aware of the involvement of gentry in such practices as *guiji* [whereby landowners registered land in the name of another household to avoid labor service—JAF], *baolan* [proxy remittance—JAF], and the like. Thus, Yamamoto believes the establishment of the land-and-poll tax resulted in an increased poll tax on landowners and, accompanying this development, an encouragement for gentry to engage in *baolan*.

One characteristic of the Ming-Qing era was a diversification of social strata. In "Heterodoxy and Vagabondage in China"[a] (in *Chūsei*), Yasuno Shōzō examines "vagabonds" (*wulai*) primarily for the Qing period. He sees them as the bearers of "heterodoxy" (as represented by the White Lotus Sect) standing in opposition to orthodox Confucianism. Yasuno's use of the expression "orthodox-heterodox" is designed to point up a contrast between an "indigenous" peasantry and "wandering" vagabonds. In this connection one might also contrast rent or tax resistance and religious rebellion, or rice culture versus that of corn and other grains. At the basis of Yasuno's distinction lies a clear sense of regional differentiation between Jiangnan and North China.

Yasuno's picture of vagabondage differs from those of Oyama Masaaki, Kawakatsu Mamoru, and Ueda Makoto. Looking primarily at North China and Sichuan, Yasuno defines "vagabonds" as drifters who have left their native districts, and he sees their bond with religious and secret societies as inseparable. By contrast, looking mostly at Jiangnan from the mid-Ming on, Oyama, Kawakatsu, and Ueda see these "vagabonds" as a new stratum among a more stratified and socially specialized peasantry. They were violent groups of men engaged in a variety of livelihoods both in cities and in villages, often involved with local gentry and petty functionaries. Although both sides of this scholarly divide understand "vagabonds" from the perspective of the power-holders, one wonders if these two interpretations of "vagabondage" might actually result from differences in regional levels of productive capacity and economic development. If we merely reduce this to the economic distinction between "advanced" and "backward" areas, however, our research is not likely to develop further.

Kishi Kazuyuki's article, "Pearl Ponds and Pearl Pond Thieves in Guangdong during the Ming Dynasty"[b] (*Tōyō shi ronshū* 14), examines the boat people (*danmin*) who lived off the production of pearls along the Guangdong coast in the late Ming. He analyzes the activities of pearl thieves and adds that these thieves were groups of boat people, of local bandits based on Hainan Island, and of vagabonds in the Pearl River delta. Kishi argues that they maintained relationships with merchants and landlords who loaned them funds for their activities and traded in pearls. His central concern is with these "people of the sea," but one would like to know just what he wants to elucidate on the basis of his analysis.

In the area of political history, Shiroi Takashi has written two essays: "Shen Yiguan's Politics and Factional Rivalries in the Wanli 30's [1602-12]"[b] (*Shien* 122); and "On the Reforms in the Hanlin Academy of the Early Jiajing Reign"[c] (*Tōyō shi ronshū* 14). The first of these offers an analysis of the oppressive factional politics and rivalries around Shen Yiguan, senior grand secretary in the Grand Secretariat. He argues that these were political struggles between people of different regional origins: Shen and his Zhejiang group vs. bureaucrats from Shaanxi. The purge of Shen's faction after his fall was the manifestation of political demands coming from lower level officials, primarily supervising secretaries and censors. The second essay discusses increased intervention by imperial power into the personnel affairs of the Grand Secretariat and the Hanlin Academy. What one would really like to see here is an explanation, transcending individual emperors and officials, of the political structure of the Ming court in its concrete relations with the political process.

Wada Masahiro's article, "An Investigation of the Status System in Local Bureaucracy of the Ming"[d] (*Tōyō shi kenkyū* 44.1), examines the emergence of a rigid system based on the prestige of *jinshi* rank and other official positions in the Ming. He shows how this affected the appointments of local officials. He also looks at the wide recruitment of *shengyuan* (under the subsequent Qing policy of official retrenchment) and the relative rise in social status of *shengyuan* and *juren* vis à vis *jinshi*. In addition, Wada provides numerous statistical tables.

In the area of thought and literature, let me mention the following essays, though I cannot describe their content: Inoue Susumu, "The Scholarship of the Fushe"[a] (*Tōyō shi kenkyū* 44.2); Miura Shūichi, "The Young Yan Yuan"[b] (*Nihon Chūgoku gakkai hō* 37); Miura Shūichi, "The Thought of Yan Yuan"[c] (*Shūkan Tōyōgaku* 54); and Tanaka Issei, "The View of Drama Held by Late Ming Literati"[b] (*Tōyō bunka kenkyūjo kiyō* 97).

In addition, three books, each deserving separate reviews, were published: Sasaki Tatsuo, *Gen-Min jidai yōgyō shi kenkyū* (Studies in the History of Ceramics in the Yuan and Ming Periods)[a]; Hoshi Ayao, *Chūgoku shakai fukushi seisaku shi no kenkyū: Shindai no shinzaisō o chūshin ni* (Studies in the History of Chinese Social Welfare Policies: Centering on the Relief Granaries of the Qing Dynasty)[c]; and *Migami*.

Also worthy of note are three articles that appeared in the volume *Kenryoku*: Fuma Susumu, "Lü Kun's Program for the Yangjiyuan"[b]; Taniguchi Kikuo, "One Aspect of the Merging of the Land-and-Head Taxes"[c]; and Kanbe Teruo, "On *Gaitu guiliu* in the Yongzheng Period."[b].

Finally, I would like to add a word about archival materials. It is well known that a wide variety of archival documents have recently been published in Beijing and Taibei, and studies which make use of them have come out in Japan. Needless to say, these materials have enormous value as primary documents, but at the present stage we still lack a methodology for handling them. In this connection, let me point to a study that introduces the work of Zhang Weiren: Kamachi Noriko, "A Study of Qing Letter-Writing, Based on Archival Materials"[a] (*Kindai Chūgoku kenkyū ihō* 7).

Due to limitations of space I had to omit from consideration many other pieces of research. I beg forgiveness of the authors and my readers.

6

Japanese Studies of Post-Opium War China: 1985

Motono Eiichi and Sakamoto Hiroko, in *Shigaku zasshi* 95.5 (May 1986), 221-229.

Reading through publications from 1985, one is most acutely struck by the impasse confronted by research based on comparative historical perspectives. Be they Marxist or non-Marxist, studies elucidating modern Chinese history which take as a standard for comparative evaluation the history of the development of capitalism in the West and Japan have already reached their limit. In fact, the items on modern China in two major introductions to research, one published in Tokyo and one in Kyoto several years ago, were appallingly uninteresting—merely a marshalling of secondary materials and the titles of document collections and reference works, following a periodization which has not changed in the least since the publication of H. B. Morse's *The International Relations of the Chinese Empire* [publ. 1910-1918—JAF]. Clearly the energy needed to confront the radical changes that have taken place in the last ten years has evaporated from works of this sort.

Sawaya Harutsugu expressed misgivings about this scholarly stagnation in his essay, "The State of Affairs [Indicated by] the *Chūgoku shi kenkyū nyūmon* [Introduction to the Study of Chinese History, ed. Yamane Yukio]"[a] (*Shigaku zasshi* 94.3). Even more important is an essay by Uchiyama Masao based on his own research as well as the report of the students in the Department of Economics at Komazawa University: "Looking at Japan and Looking at China"[a] (in *Gendai Ajia e no shiten: Ajia gendai shi* [Approaches to Contemporary Asia: Contemporary Asian History],[a] ed. Rekishigaku kenkyūkai). Explanations of Chinese history based on comparison with "modern Europe" are losing their persuasive power not only among specialists but among younger people who are full of concern and doubts about China.

One can find as well a deep awareness of this situation in Mizuguchi Yūzō's piece of two years ago, "Isn't Our Image of Modern China Distorted?"[b] (*Rekishi to shakai* 2), but no response to Mizoguchi was to be found in the scholarly literature until this past year. Worthy of particular note among the responses was the trend to explain modern Chinese history as one part of the capitalist world system. Although as a whole we are still at a stage of trial and error, if future studies develop, perhaps they will relativize Chinese society and raise issues overlooked by previous comparative historical research. Furthermore, research from this perspective will make it more possible than before for scholars of Japanese and European history to engage in modern Chinese historical research. One characteristic of last year is that the kinds of work Japanese and European historians would like to get their hands on are indeed beginning to appear.

Also, translations of excellent work from overseas, the introduction of recent trends (such as in Ding Richu's "The Present State of Research on Modern Chinese Economic History"[a] [*Shingai kakumei kenkyū* 5]), as well as major works that make use of unpublished materials abroad, were all important products of last year's research. In a word, these directions point to changes brought about by the remarkable expansion of vision in Japanese society in recent years and the emergence of a new generation of scholars. For scholars in generations to come, the year 1985 may mark the first major turning point in Japanese studies of modern Chinese history since the end of World War II.

Proceeding from this major shift in perspective directly to a reexamination of issues leads us to a number of questions surrrounding the opening of Chinese ports, "semi-colonization," and the response of the Chinese authorities. One work which examines the first two of these three is Katō Yūzō's *Kurofune zengo no sekai* (The World at the Time of [the Arrival of Commodore Perry's] Black Ships).[e] This book is a general work concerned primarily with the opening of Japan's ports, although I cannot ultimately agree with its conclusions about the opening of China's ports. Katō sees China's foreign trade, at the time of the opening of her ports, within the framework of the well-known triangular trade involving England and India. However, as the research of Tokunaga Shōjirō and Hamashita Takeshi[1] make clear, China's foreign trade at this time formed another triangle with England and the United States. Thus, China's foreign trade must be understood in a multilateral web of accounts with these other nations. Furthermore, it has been shown that the international monetary markets were reorganized at the time of the gold rush in the 1850's, and in conjunction with this development China changed from a silver exporter because of the opium trade to a silver importer through a massive increase in the tea and raw silk thread trades.[2] Why did Katō completely fail to examine what had caused these developments?

Katō next offers a comparison between the Ansei Treaty and the Tianjin and Beijing Treaties. He terms Ansei a negotiated treaty and the latter two the results of defeat in war. There are basic distinctions between the two treaties, regarding (1) indemnities and cession of territory, (2) the difficulty of treaty revision, (3) the extent of intervention in domestic politics, and particularly (4) the presence or absence of a clause concerning the opium trade. These, he argues, largely explain the diametrically opposite fates met by China and Japan under the same unequal treaty system. As the major work of William T. Rowe on commerce and society in 19th century Hankou demonstrates, the unequal treaties never posed an obstacle to the "semi-colonization" of China by Westerners resident there.[3] The "semi-colonization" of China is not a simple issue, as Katō conceives of it, that can be explained by a rough comparative analysis of bits from various treaties. It is a major subject for research requiring explanation based on numerous concrete examples.

Shibahara Takuji's work, which is far superior to Katō's, reveals that he was fully aware of this point in his essays: "The Modern Period in East Asia"[a] (in *Kōza Nihon rekishi* [Essays on Japanese History], vol. 7, *Kindai* [Modern Period], vol.1); and "The Trade in Cotton Goods and Raw Silk and Their Backgrounds in China and Japan"[b] (*Oikonomika* 21.2-4). Not only does he offer comparisons between unequal treaties in the two countries, but Shibahara presents comparative perspectives on the reorganization of domestic industry. He looks primarily at the Chinese and Japanese import and export trade and their respective cotton and silk-reeling industries—at their financing and credit systems, and at the restructuring of the flow of commodities from the period of the opening of ports through the eve of the Sino-Japanese War of 1894-95. In his view their different national fates reflect differences in the response of their regimes and differences in the systems that necessitated their responses, and he sees China and Japan beginning to diverge in the decade of the 1880's. These painstaking works contain numerous suggestions for comparative research as well as for issues to be examined.

Yet, I cannot agree with his notion that the loans for defense in Fujian mark the point at which the Qing government became increasingly financially vulnerable in foreign relations. In the 1870's Qing finances remained sound, and the London money markets were still conservative about offering loans to China.[4] On the importance of the 1870's as the crucial turning point, one should look at Ishii Kanji's piece, "Imperialism in East Asia"[a] (in *Kōza Nihon rekishi*, vol. 8, *Kindai*, vol. 2). This is an issue which needs the serious attention of scholars of Japanese history, though at present only one scholar of Chinese history, Suzuki Tomoo, has touched on it at all.

As for articles concerned with the response of the Chinese authorities, namely the *yangwu* or early Westernization movement, we have an essay by Kubota Bunji, "Is Our Image of Modern China Distorted[a]?" (*Shichō* N. S. 16). As can be seen from his title, Kubota is offering a direct rebuttal to Mizoguchi Yūzō. He looks at the development of historical research at home and abroad, and to that extent this piece, like Chen Jian's "New

Trends in Research on the Early Westernization Movement in Chinese Historical Scholarship"[a] (*Rekishigaku kenkyū* 544), is surely an essential piece of work worthy of our attention. As a response to Mizoguchi's article, however, it is disappointing. This is because Kubota misread Mizoguchi's basic conception of "a monistic view of the popular revolution." Kubota understands this expression to mean the same thing as "research based on the materialist conception of history." He offers a harsh evaluation of the *yangwu* movement, the Hunan Army, the Huai Army, and the Beiyang Navy. From a comparative historical perspective, they incorporated modern industry and led to the emergence of a proletariat, but they lacked the policy and power structures that would have encouraged and nurtured a capitalist system. Thus, Kubota attacks Mizoguchi's positive evaluation of *yangwu*.

Mizoguchi's expression, "a monistic view of the popular revolution," however, does not simply mean "research based on the materialist conception of history." It embraces all studies which fail to "try and understand the Qing establishment historically and objectively." Accordingly, Kubota's view that judges the *yangwu* movement by the standard of its contribution to the development of Chinese capitalism and industry fits Mizoguchi's category. Furthermore, for those of us engaged in research on modern China, the notion that the *yangwu* movement failed to encourage or nurture the capitalist system in China is as self-evident as it is a stale insight. Ever since college examinations in Japan, we have accepted as given the historical fact that China, whose ports were opened in the two Opium Wars, became "a semi-colonial, semi-feudal society." By reading the same historical materials over and over again, such facts have been implanted in all students and scholars of the postwar generation. The problem is how we are to evaluate the early Westernization movement while still agreeing with this assessment. In his conclusion, Mizoguchi says that "without rushing to 'evaluations,' those of us with our many and sundry opposing views must penetrate the historical developments through historical realism, actual facts." For this reason he stresses the subjective intentions of *yangwu* officials and points [for instance] to the dual nature of *tuanlian*/clan cohesion. If we overlook this and assume a defiant attitude that "in comparison to his exaggerated title, his [i.e., Mizoguchi's] proposition is really weak" [as Kubota argues—JAF], then the debate will bring about no results, and Mizoguchi will be at no loss for a rebuttal.

In concrete terms, what would be best for developing research on the early Westernization movement? One approach, as a matter of course, would be to forage assiduously for historical documents and unearth new historical facts. An excellent example of this approach is the string of essays by Suzuki Tomoo: "A Study of Views on the Transplantation of the Modern Cotton Industry during the Era of the *yangwu* Movement"[c] (*Shichō* N. S. 16); "The Formation of Modern Industry in China and the Early Westernizers"[d]

(*Rekishigaku kenkyū* 540); "Li Hongzhang and the Transplantation of Modern Industry"[e] (in *Kikuchi*). Each of these three essays was written as a concrete critique of Mizoguchi's article from Kubota's point of view. While supplementing his own earlier theories with discoveries of new historical material in *Tsun-wan yat-bo*, *Shenbao*, and Xie Fucheng's *Yongan wen bieji*, Suzuki demonstrates subtle changes in the Westernizers' policies toward domestic capital in the early 1880's. This point fits well with the issues raised by Shibahara and Ishii, cited earlier, and is worthy of further study.

Banno Masataka's book, *Chūgoku kindaika to Ba Kenchū* (The Modernization of China and Ma Jianzhong),[a] provides another approach. He analyzes views [of men like Ma Jianzhong—JAF] concerning the training of specialists and technicians as well as the Chinese political leaders who would not listen to such views. Please look at the detailed review of this book in *Shakai keizai shigaku* (51.2) and that of Sasaki Yō in *Shigaku zasshi* (94.11). We all mourn the death of Professor Banno who left us this major piece of scholarship.

Studies on China's political structure are lagging behind. Three pieces from last year are: Ōtani Toshio, "On the Policies for Controlling Jiangnan of Tao Shu and Lin Zexu"[e] (in *Kenryoku*); Ōtani Toshio, "On the Formation of Hunanese Officials in the Late Qing Period"[f] (*Tōyō shi kenkyū* 44.2); and Murao Susumu, "Intellectuals in the Xuehaitang in Guangzhou and the Debates over Lifting the Ban on Opium or Strictly Enforcing It"[a] (*Tōyō shi kenkyū* 44.3). These essays are limited to the period of the Opium War.

Another essay that deals with Ma Jianzhong and the training of technicians in the late Qing is Marianne Bastid-Brugière's "Overseas Chinese Students in Europe in the Late Qing"[a] (*Tō-A* 213, trans. Shimada Kenji and Hase Etsuhiro). This is a fascinating piece that makes use of the documents of Prosper Giquel, the French Naval Archives, the Foreign Office Archives, and rarely seen materials uncovered by the author in Fuzhou. Unfortunately, all the notes to source materials were cut out so that the original citations are missing, and the author's name is even incorrectly written.

Other work on the early Westernizers includes: Kanbe Teruo, "Sino-British Negotiations over the Margary Affair"[c] (*Tōyō shi kenkyū* 44.2); and Sasaki Yō, "The Views of Japan Held by Early Westernizers in the Tongzhi Reign of the Qing Period"[b] (*Tōyō shi kenkyū* 44.3). In each of these cases, further work is expected. There is also translated material by Sasaki in "From the Period of the Sino-Japanese War (2)"[c] (*Kindai Chūgoku* 17).

Popular movements, of course, form one important part of modern Chinese history. Work done in this area last year was meager indeed. The only essay worthy of note was Ozawa Junko's "The Xiamen Uprising of 1852"[a] (*Shiron* 38). She argues that after the opening of Xiamen [Amoy], there developed a rivalry there between, on the one hand, Chinese merchants involved in the coolie trade which had increased and, on the other, returned overseas Chinese and compradors from Guangdong. She demonstrates that this uprising was a serious incident causing the center of the coolie trade to move from Xiamen to Shantou [Swatow] and causing the English to change their trade policy.

Aside from Ozawa's essay, one might also point to a few other articles: Fukuda Setsuo and Tsutsumi Kazuyoshi, "Pirate Activities in the Lower Yangzi Delta in the Late Qing"[b] (*Fukuoka joshi tandai kiyō* 29); Watanabe Atsushi, "Secret Societies in Modern China"[c] (in *Kikuchi*); Tessan Hiroshi, "A Study of the *Chengdu jiaoan* [Missionary Cases in Chengdu]"[c] (*Jimbun ronsō* 13) which concerns missionary cases in May 1895; and Sasaki Mamoru, "The Social Nature of the Boxer Movement in Shandong"[a] (*Minzokugaku kenkyū* 50.2) which, based on field investigations done by Shandong University researchers and by the author, treats the historical background of Boxer groups in Shandong Province. Judging by the quality of these articles, a revival of research in this area is to be yearned for.

Similarly, only a few studies have been forthcoming on the reorganization of the structure of local control at the time of the Taiping revolution. In his essay "On Pan Cengjin"[a] (*Hōsei shigaku* 37), Yamana Hirofumi discusses the career of one gentryman of Suzhou who lived in this period and the significance and limitations of his method of land division which spread as a countermeasure to rural social discontent. Takahashi Kōsuke examines the activities of commercial capital in Shanghai, in his essay "The Establishment of the Hubei [i.e., North Shanghai] Xiliu Company"[d] (*Miyajiro kyōiku daigaku kiyō* 19).

In "On Forced Labor in Shaanxi Province in the Late Qing"[b] (*Tōyō shi kenkyū* 44.3), Kataoka Kazutada uses the example of Shaanxi Province to demonstrate how changes in the forms of forced labor (institutions of taxation and *corveé*), which were implemented to maintain the communication and transport systems between Beijing and the provinces to the Northwest and the Southwest, together with the establishment of forced labor bureaus in this period, brought about strengthening of control held by local officials, gentry, and functionaries, as well as further guarantees supporting their interests.

By contrast, there has been considerable scholarly attention directed toward social and economic history and on the history of local administrative systems in the period from the first Sino-Japanese War through World War I. In the case of social and economic history, in particular, some scholars have tried to escape any comparative historical notions. The result may be seen in the limitations of Kojima Yoshio's essay, "The Village Handicraft Industry in Wujiang County, Suzhou Prefecture in the Period of the 1911 Revolution"[b] (*Keizai shūshi* 54.3). He describes how peasant domestic textile laborers in Shengzezhen, opposed to purchasing price controls, attempted to form their own industrial organization (*gongsuo*) to finance production capital without interest. They were, however, frustrated by obstructions thrown in their way by brokers (*linghu*), wholesalers (*chouzhuang*), and money stores (*qianzhuang*).

Confiscations from the peasant populations by merchant capitalists, however, go back as far as the late Ming and early Qing, and certainly reference to such confiscations alone does not elucidate the historical nature of the 1911 Revolution. Rather, the issue here is why the struggle of peasant domestic textile laborers against commercial and usury capital had to assume the form of a movement to found an industrial organization of their own at this point in time. Explaining this requires a global perspective on events from the opening of the ports in China.

Two representative examples of globally-integrated research would be: Sugihara Kaoru, "The Formation and Structure of Trade within Asia"[a] (*Shakai keizai shigaku* 51.1); and Hamashita Takeshi, "The Flow of Silver in the Scope of Modern Asian Trade"[f] (*Shakai keizai shigaku* 51.1). Examining the actual trade within Asia, Sugihara speaks of a "system based in the cotton industry" formed by Indian raw cotton production (which emerged to center stage from 1898), the Anglo-Indian textile industry, Chinese handicraft production, and the consumption of Asian cotton cloth. He then proceeds to a discussion of the sugar trade from Southeast Asia to the United States via India, China, and Japan. He argues that the collapse of the silver-based monetary system within Asia, combined with changes in the gold standard in Japan, integrated inter-Asian trade into world trade and made it more monetarily subservient to Europe and the United States.

Hamashita Takeshi's essay concerns the same subject from the perspective of the history of currencies. He argues that a variety of measures adopted by colonial banks in the face of the decline in the value of silver—changes in the forms of commercial settlements, investment activities in China, retention of a gold-based debenture, and the increased issuance of bank notes—together with the establishment of a gold exchange standard in India, the Philippines, and Indonesia and the Jencks recommendation in China—all served to stabilize the monetary order. Also, the trade between Asian countries and nations on the gold standard and the expansion of trade within Asia caused the emergence of Hong Kong and Singapore as collection and distribution centers for capital.

One study which treats colonial banks is the major work of Gonjō Yasuo, *Furansu teikokushugi to Ajia* (French Imperialism and Asia).[a] He makes use of a huge quantity of unpublished French-language documents to describe the actual workings of the Indochina Bank. This book represents the most important accomplishment in this area of research in recent years, and it deserves detailed book reviews.

Christian Daniels' essay, "The International Position of Chinese Sugar" (*Shakai keizai shigaku* 50.4), is a specialized piece of scholarship dealing with the sugar trade which Sugihara noted as so important. Taking as his main examples North China markets and the Taiwan sugar industry, he explains how the expansion by the capitalist countries of trade and capital investment in China influenced the transformation of Chinese rural handicrafts. He examines this process from the perspective of production techniques (quality) and the structure of supply. Relying on the theory of Kawakatsu Heita which stresses the use-value of commercial products, Daniels points out that, despite the sudden rise in the quantity of imported refined sugar early in the 20th century, previous sugar markets dealing primarily in white [granulated] sugar and crystal [rock] sugar did not fall apart completely. Behind the apparent formation of a two-tiered structure by the 1920's was a Chinese sugar industry limited by the scope of rural production in small-scale sugar refineries, based on a self-sufficient rural economy and on exchange relations among guild merchants, brokers, and peasants. This essay is a masterpiece making use of Customs Reports as well as unpublished materials from the Colonial Sugar Refining Company in Australia. It will surely become a basic document in this area of research.

Two further essays on the trade in commodities, as seen from the perspective of use-value are: Hata Korehito, "The Tea Trade in Modern China"[b] (in *Kikuchi*); and Kawakatsu Heita, "The Structure and Development of Asian Markets for Cotton Goods"[a] (*Shakai keizai shigaku* 51.1). Several items essential as basic research tools have recently appeared, such as: Tsunoyama Sakae and Takashima Masaaki, eds., *Maikurofirumu han ryōji hōkoku shiryō shuroku mokuroku* (A Listing of Consular Reports and Documents on Microfilm)[a]; and Nakagawa Yasuko, "A Listing of Items Concerning China in the *Tsūshō isan*"[a] (*Shingai kakumei kenkyū* 5). These works will considerably facilitate the use and study of consular reports from the Japanese Foreign Office.

One ambitious work which ingeniously fuses a perspective on China from without and from within through an examination of finances is Kuroda Akinobu's "The Structure of the Reform of Authority and Its Background"[b] (*Rekishigaku kenkyū* 547). Kuroda looks at the increase in Chinese exports at a time of an international rise in the price of primary products brought on by both the transformation of the structure of production at the core of the world economy and by the rise in nominal wages in urban areas. He argues that these two developments with respect to exports, together with later monetary reforms, were the response of China's powerholders at the time of the 1898 Reform Movement as well as the ultimate cause of its failure. This is a fascinating thesis and there are many points to be learned here, but this essay is not without problems. Is not explaining late Qing domestic politics solely on the basis of trends in export trade overstressing the importance of exports? China's trade balance sheet at this time was thoroughly in the red, and the influence exerted on Chinese society and economy by imports was, it seems, much greater. Furthermore, Kuroda does not touch on the influences of loans and investments made by the Western powers in China at the time of the "rights recovery controversy." These will be tasks for Kuroda in the future.

Kuroda's was not the only essay over the past year that dealt with issues involving the Guangxu emperor's reforms. Aside from the essay by the Chinese scholar Xu Dingxin (trans. Kurahashi Masanao), "The Origins of Merchant Associations in Old China"[a] (*Aichi kenritsu daigaku bungakubu ronshū* 34), all the other pieces are concerned with local administrative institutions. Two articles discuss the local militia office in Hunan: Fujitani Kōetsu, "On the Nature of the Reform Movement in Hunan"[b] (in *Kikuchi*); and Meguro Katsuhiko, "Conditions in Late 19th Century Hunan and the Response of the Reform Clique"[b] (*Shūkan Tōyōgaku* 54). Hamaguchi Masako's "The Provincial Assembly in Zhili in the Late Qing"[a] (in *Kikuchi*) analyzes the activities of that assembly at the end of the dynasty.

In his essay "Notes on Local Political Modernization in the Early 20th Century"[a] (in *Chūgoku no kindaika to chihō seiji* [Modernization and Local Politics in China], Yokoyama Suguru offers a positive evaluation of the 1898 reform movement as an era in which a political program advocated down into the Republican period was fully planned and begun. His essay is followed in the same volume by several case studies: Morita Akira, "Local Autonomy and River Conservancy Work in Shanghai in the Late Qing"[e]; Sōda Saburō, "Reforms Prior to the 1911 Revolution and Hunan Province"[b]; and Nakayama Yoshihiro, "Political Development and National Unification in Zhejiang at the Time of the 1911 Revolution."[b] Finally, we have another essay on the early Republican years by Nakamura Jihee, "Several Problems Surrounding Rural Villages in Shanxi"[b] (in *Chūō daigaku hyakushūnen kinen ronbunshū* [Collection of Essays Commemorating the Centenary of Chūō University]).

What emerges in these studies is the great importance of the roles played by enlightened Qing officials, constitutionalist intellectuals, and conservative gentry in the promotion of local autonomy. The major work by Fujioka Kikuo, *Chō Ken to Shingai kakumei* (Zhang Jian and the 1911 Revolution),[b] stands in concert with these essays from the perspective of political history. Its 647 pages really deserve detailed book reviews.

A goodly number of essays were published last year on the occasion of the 60th anniversary of the death of Sun Zhongshan. Aside from general volumes and works of trivial exegesis, only two essays actually offered correctives to past evaluations of Sun, both dealing with the pre-World War I period: Kubota Bunji, "Sun Zhongshan's Views on Japan"[b] (in *Kikuchi*); and Terahiro Teruo, "Sun Zhongshan's Revolutionary Activities in Europe"[a] (*Ōsaka kyōiku daigaku shakai kagaku seikatsu kagaku kiyō* 33.2). Kubota demonstrates that the reason Sun had such a positive, compromising attitude toward Japan derived from the distinctive strategy of the revolutionaries who were trying to make use of conflicts among the imperialist nations to advance the cause of their own revolution. Terahiro examines the revolutionary groups Sun helped organize in Europe and the relationship Sun formed with overseas students there from Hubei, a subject very rarely discussed. Terahiro sees Sun's success in this instance as cause for the formation in Tokyo of the Tongmenghui (Revolutionary Alliance).

Kojima Yoshio has written several related essays on the Chinese students in Japan who played such a critical role in the 1911 Revolution: "Trends Among Chinese Students in Japan in the Period of the 1911 Revolution"[c] (in *Kikuchi*); "On the Chinese National Assembly (Part 4)"[a] (*Shingai kakumei kenkyū* 5); and "The 1911 Revolution and Chiba Medical School"[d] (*Chiba shigaku* 7). Many essays, such as the following two, examine the history of certain institutions prior to the acceptance of Chinese students in them: Nakamura Tadashi, "The Seijō School and Chinese Overseas Students"[c] (in *Kikuchi*); and Kobayashi Tomoaki, "The Shinbu School and Overseas Chinese Military Students in Japan"[b] (in *Kikuchi*). These essays are all concerned with digging up historical facts, so that fresh scholarly perspectives do not emerge from this research.

Two essays examine foreign relations during the period of the 1911 Revolution: Matsumoto Takehiko, "Anti-Japanese Boycotts and Overseas Chinese in Japan"[d] (in *Kikuchi*); and Katakura Yoshikazu, "On the Ji Yulin Incident"[a] (*Tōhōgaku* 70). Yasuda Tōru's article, "China's Participation in World War I"[a] (*Keiō gijuku daigaku daigakuin hōgaku kenkyū ronbunshū* 23), deals both with China's foreign policy vis à vis Japan as well as with the domestic policies of the Duan Qirui government as they concern issues involved in China's decision to declare war on Germany and Austria when World War I erupted. The Yasuda piece sheds light on the national power and diplomacy of the Beiyang militarists and deserves our attention.

Finally, I would like to conclude my portion of this review article[5] with the work of two eminent scholars concerned with problems in Sino-Japanese relations: Yamane Yukio, "Yuan Shikai and the Japanese"[e] (*Shakai kagaku tōkyū* 30.3); and Nakamura Tadashi, "Kanō Jigorō and Yang Du"[d] (*Shingai kakumei kenkyū* 5). These articles analyze the thought and activities of Banzai Rihachirō and Kanō Jigorō, respectively, men who had a major impact on the history of Sino-Japanese relations in their capacities, respectively, as military advisor to Yuan Shikai and welcomer of numerous Chinese students in Japan. Yamane and Nakamura point out the sad fact that, although both Banzai and Kanō individually hoped for the best possible neighborly relations with China, insofar as they followed the national interests and ruling ideology of Japan at the time, a wall stood in the way of their sincerity and action. It's easy to point out and criticize the limitations of such men from our present perspective. However, at present when the largest anti-Japanese demonstrations in China (at least since the Cultural Revolution) by the postwar generation in China have taken place on the occasion of Prime Minister Nakasone's visit to the Yasukuni Shrine, am I alone in supposing that this wall will again rise as an obstruction to Japanese leaders in the political, financial, and bureaucratic world?

Although we have seen critiques of the overemphasis on political matters in studies of modern Chinese thought, the orientation toward an internal analysis which has become rather apparent in recent years now offers us concrete results. This part of the present review article, as the first attempt to treat the history of thought independently, requires a certain leeway in the year of publication of the essays to be considered.

Let us look at two studies of individual thinkers by Ogata Yasushi, "Wang Guowei or Forms of Leaping"[a] (Byōtōō 4); and "Yan Fu and John Stuart Mill's Logic"[b] (Chūtetsubun gakukai hō 10). In the first of these, Wang Guowei is portrayed as locating the essence of reality in non-transcendental values different from those derived from experience; and so rejecting temporality, he falls into an atemporal confusion. Ogata sees Wang's effort to overcome this chronic disease as a "mode" of conceptual leap, revealed in his distinctive notions of ethics, responsibility, "ancient elegance," and institutions. The second of Ogata's articles offers a perspective toward an overall understanding of Yan Fu's irrational sense of the mystery at the heart of life. He sees Yan, in Mingxue (Yan's translation of Mill), using formal logic to reach an insight into knowledge of life, thus irrationalizing the inductive method based on energy/reason. He relates this to Yan's views that translations are accomplished through an internal language that evokes universal feelings.

Although there is a danger in using literary conceptual devices, as we have here, Ogata maintains the view that insofar as thought becomes an act of writing we need to reconstruct in conceptual form the universe of personal completion within written works themselves. Ogata raises these issues to challenge previous studies both in method and in content. The point, raised in the title of the article about Wang Guowei, that we must take seriously forms of thought, was argued by the late Nishi Junzō, who opened a path toward the analysis of modern thought from the perspectives of both the individual and the transcendent whole in China.

Kobayashi Takeshi has written an essay entitled "On Zhang Binglin"[a] (Kyōto sangyō daigaku ronshū 12.2). He tries to elucidate Zhang's understanding of the world through an explanation of Zhang's theory of language. Looking at Zhang's emphasis on the symbolic weight of written characters which qualitatively distinguishes them from spoken language or parole, Kobayashi organically analyzes Zhang's concept of wen [language] as linked to the zhi [substance, quality] of the real world, and Zhang's positivism which attached importance to things individually. On the basis of this analysis, Kobayashi notes that Zhang's emphasis on the written word, as an issue in culture, leads to a fixation on the intellectually privileged stratum and a reification of "tradition." By contrast, Ogata's article (discussed below) dealing with the theory of evolution, offers a different view of Zhang. Ogata emphasizes Zhang's observation that prior to the written word, spoken language symbolized the shared emotions of a people. The close tie between the Chinese language and the essence of Chinese culture [i.e., *wen*—JAF] demonstrates that we need take such an approach seriously.

Satō Shin'ichi has just completed the third and final segment, a long essay: "On Zheng Guanying (3)"[b] (*Hōgaku* 49.2), probably the first full-scale study of Zheng's thought [in Japanese—JAF]. Satō argues that the chapter of Zheng's work, *Shengshi weiyan* (Warnings to a Seemingly Prosperous Age), entitled "Daoqi" (The Way and Technique) which deals with the *tiyong* problem was merely an initial form of self-defense. The core of the text, according to Satō, lies in the chapter entitled "Jiaoyang" (Education). It describes the history of the "development" of mankind from hunting and agriculture to scientific society, and locates the intrinsic reason for China's backwardness in the ruinous decline of scholarship and education.

Working from this basis, Satō explains various other chapters of Zheng's book which advocate diversification and specialization of learning (and, as a result, the dissolution of the tradition of scholars or bureaucrats) as a means of establishing the groundwork for the state at the commercial and scientific stage of development. Satō also treats Zheng's ideas on representative government and popular rights which were to guarantee that "commercial wars" be under the rule of "international law." He notes as well that Zheng pointed out the first failures in the revivalist strain of reform in the late Qing. Zheng's views on popular rights and social evolution anticipated intellectual outlooks in China after the loss of the Sino-Japanese War: he was a model for the next generation. Zheng's ideas are especially fascinating in view of the dual intellectual development one sees in Tan Sitong's notion that "benevolence *(ren)* equals equality and learning *(xue)* equals science," and the May Fourth period's subsequent stress on Science and Democracy.

In his essay "The Introduction of Western Learning by Protestant Missionary Martin and His Chinese Writings"[b] (*Shidoku* 11), Yoshida Tora discusses the man who introduced international law to China. Martin believed that the enlightenment of China through the spread of Western learning would occur with the growth of Christian missionary work at which he labored hard.

The first full-length study [in Japan] of Kang Youwei recently appeared: Sakaide Yoshinobu, *Kō Yūi* (Kang Youwei).[c] I have already written a review of it for the journal *Chūgoku kenkyū geppō* (450).

Among other outstanding essays in intellectual history were: Ogata Yasushi [different author, different characters—JAF], "The Intellectual Position of the Theory of Evolution and Its Consequences in the Late

Qing"[a] (Chūtetsubun gakkai hō 9); Kondō Kuniyasu, "Chinese Utopia: Datong"[b] (in Yume to bijon [Dream and Vision], ed. Kimura Shōzaburō); and Kobayashi Takeshi, "Chivalry in the Late Qing"[b] (Kyōto sangyō daigaku ronshū 4.4).

Ogata's article begins with a discussion of Zhang Binglin's dualistic theory of evolution (in the first decade of the 20th century) in which one finds both irreversible progress (in the world at large) and possible reversibility (in China). The evolutionary process of change contrasts with the unchanging and essential character of an ethnic group. He looks also at Hegel's laws of evolution. He contrasts Zhang's formulation with the monistic evolutionary theories characterized by a unidirectional progressive quality that one finds in the work of Kang Youwei, Yan Fu, and others. From here he looks at the conception of the individual held by Lu Xun who departed from these earlier notions of evolution and imagined an evolution of consciousness within races, a process inherent in the development of society. According to Ogata, Li Dazhao changed the basis of this configuration from the ethnic group to the peasantry as a social stratum. By seeing the peasant as a universal evolutionary agent, he subverted the dualistic notion of evolution and reunified evolutionary theory.

Kondō discusses the negative and positive aspects of the concepts of equality in "datong" with particular attention to the Taipings, Kang Youwei, Sun Zhongshan, and Mao Zedong. Kobayashi tries to locate the collective, subjective consciousness linked to the formation of a "nation" that lay behind the personal sacrifices and chivalrous actions stimulated by the doubts of late Qing literati concerning their place in the world. He sees a kind of coexistence between an Asian "ethos of shared suffering" and the Western idea of individualism (independence without fear).

There is considerable room for debate with both Ogata's explanatory scheme of a transition from monistic to dualistic evolutionary theory, as well as with Kobayashi's parallel understanding of the coexistence of Asian and Western elements. Yet, when we look at the mutual inter-relations of evolutionary theory, datong, and the idea of chivalry, in light of such latent themes as the individual and the whole in modern and contemporary times or the manner in which Marxism was accepted into China, we probably need also to examine their relationships with lay Buddhism in China.

In addition we have one joint work which is the product of a Chinese scholar's long period of stay in Japan and a Japanese scholar's work in China: Tang Zhijun and Kondō Kuniyasu, Chūgoku kindai no shisōka (Modern Chinese Thinkers).[a] It deals mostly with Kang Youwei and Zhang Binglin. I think it might have been a more significant work if the two authors could have found a method of discussion to confront their basic differences frankly and directly, but this sort of criticism should be the responsibility of specialized reviews of the book.

7

Ming-Qing Studies in Japan: 1986

Satō Fumitoshi, in *Shigaku zasshi*
96.5 (May 1987), 219-225.

In his notes from the Ming History Conference held in Tangkouzhen, Huangshan city, Anhui in October 1985, Mori Masao (*Mindai shi kenkyū* 14) describes how lively discussion was sparked by Li Wenzhi's analysis of the "extended duration" of Chinese feudal society. The question was raised concerning the responsibility of Ming historical studies to elucidate this issue, especially because "feudalism" as a remnant of the past remains present in socialist China even as that nation presses ahead with the Four Modernizations. The conventional theory in the People's Republic holds that, through the abolition of feudal landholding during the land reform campaigns and the establishment of peasant landownership, the traditional structure of rural control was completely transformed. However, this theory is a purely political principle. The task of actually understanding the nature of the rural power structure on the basis of regional and historical variations has yet to be carried out thoroughly.

Two articles based on recent field work in the People's Republic may fill this gap. They deal with various historical aspects of Chinese society which survive today. Although both pieces are primarily concerned with the contemporary period, the phenomena examined date back to the Ming and Qing and are analyzed as they develop from the Communist revolution to the present. Ueda Makoto's essay, "How Cohesive Forces Function in the Village"[c] (2 parts, *Chūgoku kenkyū geppō* 455, 456), is based on fieldwork in the village of Qinyong, Yin County, Zhejiang. He argues that the patterns by which Japanese have understood the nature of rural Chinese society (such as *kyōdōtai* or communitarian bonds) differ enormously from the realities of Chinese villages. He examines the formation of networks of lineage ties, regional bonds, and administrative organization; and he looks at their development from the mid-Ming to the present. On the basis of this analysis, he claims that these networks were not completely internal to a single village but extended well beyond it.

Miki Satoshi has written "Land Revolution and the *Xiangzu*"[b] (in *Henkakki*). It deals with the *xiangzu* [local lineage], which have been discussed by Professor Fu Yiling in elucidating the nature of rural Chinese society. He takes as a case study a "liberated area" [from the revolutionary civil war] on the border of southern Jiangxi and western Fujian, and he examines the dissolution of the local *xiangzu* in the process of the land revolution during 1927-33. He describes how a remnant form of the *xiangzu* continued to exist into the 1950's. It was Yang Guozhen who applied Fu Yiling's view of the *xiangzu* to an understanding of landownership in the Ming-Qing period. For Yang's views, one should consult an essay concerning him which appeared in the journal *Nagoya daigaku Tōyō shi kenkyū hōkoku* (11). The fact that there were numerous articles on clan and lineage over the past year reflects this direction to research.

Landownership Relations

In two articles, Mori Masao offers a new perspective on his own studies of "official lands" (*guantian*): "On *Jimo* Land in the Early Ming"[d] (*Tōhō gakuhō* 58); "The Formation of *Jimo* Land in the Jiangnan Area in the Early Ming"[e] (*Nagoya daigaku bungakubu kenkyū kiyō ronshū* 95 [shigaku] 32). These essays deal with issues concerning state-owned lands in the late Yuan and early Ming which were not developed in the debate over the views of Nishijima Sadao concerning official lands. That debate provided the starting point for postwar Japanese studies of Ming-Qing social and economic history. This new perspective also aims at reinvestigating the old thesis of Professor Kitamura, who withdrew his theory concerning official lands in the late Yuan and early Ming when criticized by Kojima Kazuo. Kitamura had held that, through Zhu Yuanzhang's policy on official lands, the *haozu* landlord system of the Song and Yuan eras was transformed into a state landlord system, a yet higher form of landlordism. Mori also takes a fresh look at the relationship between the late Yuan peasant rebellions and landlord power.

Mori points out that "official lands" in Jiangnan in the early Ming were a composite of three land systems: Song-Yuan official lands carried over from that time, lands ownerless or abandoned due to rebellion and incorporated into the state system, and *jimo* lands. He pays particular attention to the system of *jimo* lands, or those subject to official confiscation and redistribution. In the process by which Zhu Yuanzhang established a unified regime, three types of land confiscation took place: by local bullies of the Zhang Shicheng ilk, by migrants or the rural rich for unjust economic gain, and by bureaucrats in numerous cases of graft. As a result, there was a certain redistribution from the rural rich to the poor—principally from landlords to tenants whose mutual relations had been at best poor in the local society of the late Yuan and early Ming. Mori argues that this development was due to the emergence of new owner-cultivators, as former poor peasants paid official levies on *jimo* lands; and because the newly rising landlords, replacing

MING-QING STUDIES IN JAPAN: 1986 81

the rural rich, were not people from whom it was possible to extract high land rent. This point was touched off by the latest scholarly work in China which Mori has incorporated.

We would hope for further research on the relationship between the landlord system of the Song-Yuan and the early Ming regime, as well as on the relationship between the Song and Yuan landlord system and locally-resident landlords of the early Ming. We would also like to see studies of the various aspects of the national landownership system, which continued as long as autocratic power continued; this includes research on other types of official lands, such as imperial manors, princely manors, lands for meritorious relatives, banner lands, official lands, and the like. On tilling the fields of T'ai-ho-shan, lands privately owned by the Ming imperial house, Ishida Kenji's essay, "On the Economic Basis of T'ai-ho-shan in the Ming Dynasty"[a] (in *Ran no kōzu*), attempts an analysis of tillers, tenants, and supervising central military officials in T'ai-ho-shan.

Hamashima Atsutoshi has published two articles in this area: "A Short Study of the 'Master-Servant' Bond"[e] (in *Nakamura*); and "Landlord-Tenant Relations and the Legal System in the Ming and Qing Eras"[f] (in *Henkakki*). They concern the question of how the law treated the landlord-tenant system, and they examine the legal basis for judgments concerning rent resistance and rent arrears in the Ming and Qing periods. Hamashima concludes by describing a two-tiered legal structure, for there was no officially recognized landlord-tenant relationship in state law. However, in courts at the subprefectural and county levels, where the law was implemented, the conception of a "master-servant bond" operated. In particular, this master-servant relationship existed within the scope of a status hierarchy supported by customary practice and ritual and under the control of resident landlords who were supported by Zhu Yuanzhang's regime. Cases which dealt with rent resistance and arrears, he argues, did not speak of hired hands and commoners when discussing tenants under contract; rather, their legal position was based on the ritual order. These two pieces of work are ambitious in trying to incorporate previous work on Chinese legal history while considering pre-modern class, status, and law as well as the relationship between the Chinese landlord system and the autocratic power of the state.

A third work, by Koguchi Hikota, shows that although judicial precedent was not formally recognized, in actuality it functioned as a basis for law. See his "The Legal Basis of Judicial Precedent in Criminal Trials in Qing China"[a] (*Tōyō shi kenkyū* 45.2).

We move now to research on the one-field two-owners (*yitian liangzhu*) system. In his essay "*Chengjia* and *guotou* on Chongming Island"[b] (*Chiba daigaku hōgaku ronshū* 1.1), Shiga Shūzō offers an overall evaluation of Terada Hiroaki's work on this form of land tenure as well as a new explanation for understanding *chengjia* and *guotou* in the case of Chongming Island.[1] Shiga argues that the reason Terada identified *maijia* with land rights and presented a confusing picture of the three sorts of surface rights (*chengjia*, *guotou*, and *dingshou*) is that he misunderstood *chengjia*. *Chengjia* cannot simply be seen as the tenant's right to rent reduction and a return of profit for labor rendered, but must also take into account the right to a profit of one-third of the autumn rent (a sum originally fixed as part of the land allotment). Thus, when the possessor of *chengjia*, as an "owner" of the topsoil, entrusted the management and working of his land to another, *chengjia* metamorphized into subsoil rights and became unified with *maijia*; but *guotou*—namely, lands paid for in *guotouyin*[2] when one tenant farmer replaced a previous one—continued as topsoil rights. From the Qianlong period on, sources for generating *chengjia* dried up due to changes in the laws regarding land reclamation; and a new topsoil system emerged different from *guotou* and called *dingshou*. The latter was much like the bond-rent or *ya-tsu*[3] which subsoil owners—who held full landownership rights on new polder lands—levied from tenants. Shiga's understanding of *chengjia* gives it a quality that made systemic adjustment possible.

Kishimoto Mio's essay, "The Conception of Landownership in the *Zuhe*"[a] (*Chūgoku—shakai to bunka* 1), analyzes the essential view of landownership in Tao Xu's text *Zuhe*, and through this, Tao's theory of the legitimacy of rent reduction. She also discusses the one-field two-owners system upon which Tao's work was based. According to Kishimoto, Tao held that topsoil owners were tenant farmers, and thus rent reduction was possible because they were " 'co-holders' of the same sort" as subsoil owners. She sees the facts that tenant farmers' income fell below even hired tillers and that they still bought topsoil rights at high prices to be based on a rationalization by the poor peasantry (a recognition that the guarantee of their wages, or even less than what they earned, was superior to the instability of being without work). This, she argues, differs from the principle that values subsoil as investment; on the land market, the two would not have been in competition.

In another article, "Life in Local Society in the Early Qing, as Seen in the *Linianji*"[b] (*Shigaku zasshi* 95.6), Kishimoto analyzes the *Linianji*, a chronological autobiography of Yao Tinglin, an intellectual of urban Jiangnan who survived the tumultuous Ming-Qing transition. She looks at the possibilities for diversity as well as the insecurity in Yao's employment record—three years in commerce, nine years as agricultural manager of various crops, ten years as a yamen clerk, and thirty years as owner-cultivator and teacher in a family school. With this material as background, she examines the collapse of the Ming social order and, in reaction against this, the strengthening of social cohesion based on local autonomy and self-help. The Qing regime, she argues, sought to end this local autonomy and to reinstitute the public order of a centralized authority.

Kawakatsu Mamoru's "Wheat-Rent Practices in Jiangnan in the Qing Period"[d] (in *Nakamura*) verifies, on the basis of tenant contracts and rent agreements, the maintenance of rent collection in the form of wheat-rent (which had existed since the Chongzhen era of the late Ming). In another article, "Tenancy Relations on the Lands of the Cai Jingyu Family Hall in the 19th Century"[e] (*Shien* 123), Kawakatsu analyzes the various registers for rent and the like of the landlord Cai family from Jingui County, covering the Daoguang, Tongzhi, and Guangxu periods of the Qing. These materials are held in the library of the Research Institute for Humanistic Sciences of Kyoto University. On the basis of his examination, he attempts to describe 19th century Chinese landlordism as it really was. Unfortunately, the analysis stops midstream and the last half adds little to the discussion.

Bureaucracy and the Examination System

In an essay entitled "The Political Background to the Reform of the Examination System in the Ming"[c] (*Tōhō gakuhō* 58), Danjō Hiroshi argues that with the creation of the *nanbei juan* (in 1425) and the *nanbeizhong juan* (in 1427)—both local systems for selecting officials and for choosing scholars to sit for the metropolitan examinations as part of the Ming examination system—the route toward the establishment of a Southerners' regime was cut off. Danjō describes in systematic detail the equalization of North and South carried out in the area of bureaucratic recruitment. This was an epochal step, he argues, for the Ming and Qing periods.

The Korean scholar Oh Keum-sung (O Gŭm-sŏng) has written a piece entitled "On the Social Movement of *shenshi* in the Ming (Part 1)"[a] (*Mindai shi kenkyū* 14, trans. Yamane Yukio). In it he describes how the rules for bureaucratic appointment in the Ming, implemented simultaneously along three channels, enabled *jinshi*[4], *juren*, *jiansheng*, and *liyuan* to gain positions through official recommendation in the early Ming. He also demonstrates the special esteem in which *jiansheng* were held and their relations within these various strata of the scholar-officialdom. Oh has also published a volume entitled *Chungguk kûnse sahoe kyôngje sa yôn'gu* (Studies in Modern Chinese Social and Economic History).[b]

Pan Liangzhi's "A Critical Discussion of the Censorial System for Officials in the Early Ming"[a] (*Mindai shi kenkyū* 14) argues that Zhu Yuanzhang's policy of "nourishing the people" in the devastated society of the early Ming as well as his strict examination and promotion-demotion policies for officials facilitated successful reformation of corrupt bureaucrats.

In his article "An Analysis of the Administrative Thought of the Yongzheng Emperor of the Qing (Parts 1 and 2)"[a] (*Yahata daigaku ronshū* 37.1-2, 37.3), Liang Xizhe (trans. Wada Masahiro) analyzes the success attained by the Yongzheng Emperor in administrative reforms of utmost importance to the state's rule.

In addition, the Tōyō shi kenkyūkai (East Asian Studies Association) has published *Yōsei jidai no kenkyū* (Studies of the Yongzheng Period).[a] A draft index to the Vermillion Edicts of the Yongzheng Emperor has been published, with commentary by Ono Kazuko. This tool for specialized research appears in the journal *Tōyō shi kenkyū* (45.3). Both are enormously welcome contributions to scholarship.

Let us turn next to work on the purchase of official posts. Wataru Masahiro's essay, "An Overview of the Purchase of Bureaucratic Posts in the Early Ming"[b] (*Shūkan Tōyōgaku* 56), looks at the increase in the number of *jiansheng* obtained through purchase which was encouraged in the Jingtai reign of the Ming and continued without limitation from the Jiajing period. He sees this as one indication of the formation of the gentry. We still need to examine the gentry's relations with various other strata of bureaucrats and examination candidates.

In his article "Purchase of Office in the Early Qing"[a] (*Shundai shigaku* 66), Yamada Kōichirō agrees that during the Rebellion of the Three Feudatories (1673-81) military exigencies led to the purchase of a large number of bureaucratic posts by men from a variety of classes. However, many will be unable to accept that this situation continued past 1692, after the conclusion of the rebellion. Therefore, he demonstrates how the aftermath of this policy was to create an oversupply of personnel blocking the principal path to official position.

In "Bureaucratic Present-Giving in the Qing"[c] (*Tōhoku gakuin daigaku ronshū* 16), Kōsaka Masanori examines the presentation of gifts by officials (*kuisong*),[5] a private principle which supported the inner workings of bureaucratic society. In particular, he analyzes the case of Wu Cunli, who was cashiered as governor of Jiangsu for paying out a "debt" in excess of 400,000 taels of silver in the late Kangxi period. Although this *kuisong* was of a sort labeled "customary" by Professor Abe Takeo, Kōsaka cites many highly-placed persons among the recipients of *kuisong* and sees the case of Wu Cunli in relation to the power struggles at the time of the accession of the Yongzheng Emperor.

Saeki Yūichi's essay, "One View of Yamen Functionaries in the Ming-Qing Transition"[b] (in *Nakamura*), makes use of the same text as Kishimoto Mio, the *Linianji* of Yao Tinglin, and analyzes Yao's years as a yamen clerk (*xuli*). He argues that becoming a subofficial functionary of this sort was a separate way for intellectuals to enhance the social mobility of their families. If, however, they sought to carry on affairs without paying their "customary dues" (*lougui*) to the local elite, they perforce had to enter the regular officialdom.

Political History and Social History

In her article "Shanxi Merchants and Zhang Juzheng"[c] (*Tōhō gakuhō* 58), Ono Kazuko analyzes the groups of officials from Shanxi Province who served in one wing of the government under Zhang Juzheng. As background she examines Shanxi merchants who lived parasitically, as salt merchants, off the state and who wielded enormous influence in managing privileged commercial enterprises. Their opportunity for a footing within Zhang's regime emerged when they took over the leadership in peace talks with the Altan Khan in 1571. Thereafter, armed with this rationale, they secured influence over policy decisions concerning political reform under Zhang Juzheng. We would like to have a study of the intertwining of the economic and political processes at work here.

The *xiangyue* (community covenant) and *baojia* (community self-defense) systems, in use since the mid-Ming era, have in the past been seen as supplementary to the declining *lijia* (community self-monitoring) system, especially the *lilaoren* (community elder) system. Inoue Tōru takes up this issue in two articles: "The World of Huang Zuo's *Taiquan xiangli*"[a] (*Tōyō gakuhō* 67.3-4); and "The Ideology of 'Community Covenants'"[b] (*Nagoya daigaku Tōyō shi kenkyū hōkoku* 11). He analyzes the political ideas and ideology of community covenants in the *Taiquan xiangli*, and he argues that the *lilaoren* system was qualitatively different from the ideology of community covenants. The first of these two systems served as local administrative assistance to the state and excluded low-level local officials. The latter included these local officials, local scholars, and the populace; it avoided state participation; and it carved out a self-regulating operation under the direction of the head of community compact groupings (*yuezhang*). These essays now complete Inoue's continuing work on the *baojia* system.

In the late Ming and early Qing, previously divided Jiangnan lineages were moving in the direction of unity. In his essay "On the Function of Ritual Theater in the Organizational Forms of Eastern Zhejiang Clans in the Qing Dynasty"[c] (*Tōyō shi kenkyū* 44.4), Tanaka Issei points out the huge role played by ritual theater in ancestral temples.

Morita Akira, in his "The Shi Lineage of Jinjiang, Fujian Province in the Late Ming and Early Qing"[f] (*Shakai keizai shigaku* 52.3), argues that the basis for the Shi family's development of Taiwan lay in their clan unity and their accumulation of experience and technical knowledge in Benguan (Jinjiang County), prior to their going to Taiwan.

In her essay "The Taizhou School in the Salt Fields"[a] (*Tōhō gakuhō* 58), Mori Noriko discusses the social worlds of Wang Xinzhai [Wang Gen] and other members of the Taizhou school whose thinking had been formed on the basis of experiences gained in private salt dealings and in the Liuliu-

Liuqi Uprising. She argues that the people at the core of the Taizhou group were local social reformers at the boundary between the populace and the intellectual class. These people wanted to strengthen clan unity and to conserve the salt fields, and they resisted the annexation and intrusion of outside authority by means of violence or other strong-arm tactics.

Suzuki Tomoo's piece, "The Offering of Incense in Worship in Hangzhou by Peasants from Jiangsu and Zhejiang in the Ming and Qing Periods"[f] (*Shikyō* 13), analyzes the historical character of incense offerings in Hangzhou by Jiangsu and Zhejiang peasants, a remarkable phenomenon from the late Ming forward. As small commercial producers, peasants continually made pilgrimages to Guangyin temples, he argues, in order to organize incense groups, carry on commercial transactions, and spread technology.

On the relations between the state, local society, and the people concerning activities on behalf of foundlings in Suzhou and Songjiang in the Qing period, Fuma Susumu has written two fascinating and descriptive essays: "The Management of Foundling Homes and Local Society in Songjiang in the Qing"[c] (*Tōyō shi kenkyū* 45.3); and "Foundling Projects of the Early Qing"[d] (*Toyama daigaku jimbun gakubu kiyō* 11). In the early Qing, projects on behalf of foundlings were begun in large cities of the Yangzi delta, but these were privately operated, with local contributions, by benevolent societies which linked the urban gentry with the local populace. However, with the expansion of the reach of these projects (from the market town, to the county, to the administrative capital), there developed the dangers that philanthropic acts would be converted into something compulsory and that such projects would become a means of fund-raising. What began as voluntary contributions from these people became voluntary contributions from land revenues and merchant guilds; and in the Daoguang period, "official contributions" began to be exacted as a surcharge on landowners. Fuma analyzes the interjection of official control as foundling projects based on private initiative expanded, and he includes issues of local autonomy within his purview.

Susan Mann's essay (trans. Kishimoto Mio), "The Position of Widows in Qing Society"[a] (*Ochanomizu shigaku* 29), examines a new area of research: the lives of widows of the Qing period in relation to their families, Chinese society, and the state.

Taxation and Labor Service Systems, Commerce and Markets

Let me first happily announce the publication of Iwami Hiroshi's *Mindai yōeki seido no kenkyū* (A Study of the Labor Service System of the Ming Dynasty).[a] We anticipate full-length reviews.

Concerning ceramics production at Jingdezhen, which was responsible for imperial porcelains, Sakuma Shigeo argues as follows in his essay, "The Production of Jingdezhen Ceramics in the Early Qing"[b] (*Tōyō tōji* 14). From the Jiajing period of the Ming on, official kilns alone were unable to fill the vast number of orders for imperial ceramics; there emerged a system of officially-built private kilns, which were relied upon for part of this ceramic production. Sakuma also notes the further development of [purely] private kilns. Between the mid-Kangxi period and the end of the Qianlong era, this Qing system of publicly subsidized kilns reached a high point. With the growth of private kilns based on specialization, the relative importance of the system of officially-built private ceramic production grew, and at the official kilns hired laborers replaced compulsory laborers.

There are still many unresolved points concerning the *jiaoxiang*, one of the three surtaxes levied by the late Ming government to provision its troops. Yoshio Hiroshi has written "On Yang Sichang's Plan for the *jiaoxiang* in the Late Ming"[c] (*Tōhō gakuhō* 58). As the basis for an overall Ming strategy against roving bandits, Yang attempted to implement a plan for a tripartite surtax and for the appointment of a new minister to oversee these surtaxes. The common aim of this triple policy was a "delivery from the gentry," and this was based on his experiences in Changde Prefecture, Hunan Province.

Nakamura Jihee's "Fishing Levies in the Early Ming and Local Evasion by Officials of the Fishing Tax Offices"[c] (*Chūō daigaku bungakubu kiyō* 31) discusses: the fishing taxes levied by the Fishing Tax Office of the early Ming which inherited similar institutions from the Yuan; and the local evasion by officials belonging to Fishing Tax Offices, a system promulgated in 1382.

There is also Suzui Masataka's article, "On the *Bianshen* System[6] and the *Qiding* Plan of the Early Qing"[a] (*Yamagata daigaku shigaku ronshū* 6). He examines the *qiding* proposal which was a poll tax of the early Qing period.

Masui Tsuneo's new book, *Chūgoku no gin to shōnin* (Silver and Merchants in China),[a] offers us a glimpse of pre-modern Chinese society and the world of merchants through the history of silver.

Although the activities of Xin'an merchants in the late Ming are well known, scarcely anything is known of the activities of Jiangnan merchants in the mid-Ming. Hamashima Atsutoshi's article, "On Jiangnan Merchants in the Mid-Ming Period"[g] (*Shihō* 20), introduces this issue. He argues that Jiangnan delta landlords who directly managed agriculture did not necessarily profit from investments in land or from agricultural management and land development (of polders). During the slack season, these landlords worked as traveling merchants, and, as a result, he claims, new markets and commercialization advanced.

On the antagonistic and dependent relationships surrounding rice in the Liang-Guang provinces during the Qing dynasty, we have Inada Seiichi's "A Study of the *Ximi dongyun*"[a] (*Tōhōgaku* 71). His analysis shows that in the

Qianlong era a system was established for the flow of Guangxi rice into Guangdong via three routes: Guangdong merchants, the *beidonggu* system[7] and Ever-Normal Granaries, and the state purchase of grain on the market [*caimai*] by Guangdong authorities. He also describes how the worsening of rice-growing conditions in Guangxi became a structural problem.

Kawakubo Teirō's essay, "A Study of Participation in Government during the Qing"[a] (*Shūkan Tōyōgaku* 55), clarifies how the Qing introduced and implemented Chinese-style institutions for the gathering and marketing of jinseng, the local speciality of Northwest China.

Rebellions

In his article, "On *Tuzei* [Local Bandits] in the Mid-Ming Period"[a] (in *Ran no kōzu*), Imaminato Yoshinobu analyzes the activities of one such bandit surnamed Ye from the Nangong region, where roving bandits gathered and the state found it difficult to extend its control. Throughout China, such "local bandits" could become local bosses who operated in a zone of influence between officials and the populace. By sheltering and making use of roving bandits, Ye became a property owner and a fence for stolen goods; he formed a strong private army and came to head a powerful family which paid no land tax to the government. The Ming was definitely antagonistic toward him, yet it also sought to coopt him as a military leader. However, when he became a major influence on local officials, the Ming concluded an agreement with another local bandit, an enemy of Ye's, and broke up his power base.

Taniguchi Kikuo's essay, "The Popular Uprising at Dongyang"[d] (*Tōhō gakuhō* 58), describes the uprising led by the "student" (*zhusheng*) Xu Du against the tyranny of the county magistrate in Dongyang County, Zhejiang Province during the collapse of the Ming. Xu Du made contacts with Qi Biaojia and Zuo Guangxian, who were trying to reorganize other private military forces to defend the Ming dynasty. Later he surrendered to his old friend Chen Zilong, but under pressure from men such as Jiang Yingjia, a local gentryman of Jinxiang County, Xu Du was executed by Zuo Guangxian. Through an examination of this one popular uprising, Taniguchi looks at the activities of the Donglin and Fushe groups surrounding Xu Du, and he examines the weaknesses of the Southern Song resistance movement caused by the opposition of powerful local gentry and the influence of eunuchs.

Sakai Tadao has written an article, "*Mang* and *Liumang* [Vagrants] in Chinese History"[a] (in *Ran no kōzu*), which discusses the history of vagrancy in China, including the Ming and Qing eras.

In his piece "The Movements of the Shimabara Rebellion as Reported to the Qing Court"[b] (*Kansai daigaku Tōzai gakujutsu kenkyū kiyō* 19), Matsuura Akira deals with how the Qing, following the conquest of China, gained information concerning the rebellion in Daoyuan from the Korean tribute-bearers to the court.

Yamada Masaru's essay, "Immigrant Society in the Qing Period"[a] (*Shirin* 69.6), fills in gaps in this area of research. He raises issues concerning the settlement of immigrants and the formation of local communities. At the height of the Qianlong period, immigrants primarily from Guangdong formed villages on the basis of common place of origin. With the emergence of powerful immigrant landlords, who were successful at land reclamation and commerce, lineage groupings around them took shape. As population and development approached a saturation point late in the Qianlong era, communities polarized between those with powerful lineages possessing ancestral temples and living in single-surname villages, and lineage groupings with a weak economic base who had no ancestral temples and who organized around the White Lotus religion.

Military Systems

One essay on the origins and development of the position of provincial governor from the military angle is Okuyama Norio's "Changes in the Governor (*Xunfu*) System in the Ming Dynasty"[a] (*Tōyō shi kenkyū* 45.2). He looks at a governor as a permanently resident local official, and he locates the origin of the office in the border defense governors of the Jingtai reign period. Initially, a censor-in-chief (*duyushi*)—who was beneath both the governor (*xunfu*, who was responsible for overseeing fiscal administration, civil government, surveillance, and military provisioning) and the military superintendent (*tidujunwu*)—was sent to the border regions. However, following public works uprisings, the two posts of provincial military commander (*tidu*) and provincial governor (*xunfu*) became unified. As the military authority of the provincial governor, who had the powers of arrest and judicial examination, became stronger and transcended that of the military commander, he also gained control over the latter's command. The provincial governor system, Okuyama argues, was then expanded into the heartland of China.

Wada Masahiro's article, "The Military Rise of a Descendant of Li Chengliang"[e] (*Yahata daigaku shakai bunka kenkyūjo kiyō* 19), offers a critical examination of Li Chengliang, a grand defender (*zhenshou*) and military commander of Liaodong, and of one of his descendants. He looks at how they overstepped the authority of the head civil officials, governors-general, and governors, and gained the principal military post in Liaodong directly tied to the emperor.

Kawachi Yoshihiro analyzes the historical nature of the Dongning guard (*wei*), which was located in the strategic territory of the Liaodong Commandant in Liaoyang, in his article, "The Dongning Guard in Liaoyang in the Ming"[a] (*Tōyō shi kenkyū* 44.4). He argues that it was a multi-ethnic city with mixed residence of Jurchens, Koreans, and Hans.

Kawagoe Yasuhiro has written two essays: "A Study of the Army Farm System in the Ming"[b] (in *Nakamura*); and "On Housemen of the Guards and Battalions System of the Ming Dynasty"[c] (*Chūō daigaku bungakubu kiyō* 31). The first of these examines how in the Ming plowing-oxen needed for the garrison lands of Liaodong were purchased from Korean peasants for a low price (bordering on requisition). In the second piece he argues that the expression *sheren* (houseman)[8] which appears on the family registers (*weixuanfu*)[9] of military officials in the guards and battalions system included descendants, legitimate and illegitimate alike, of guard and battalion officials.

Religious History

Noguchi Tetsurō's research on the White Lotus Sect has now been published as a book, *Mindai Byakurenkyō shi no kenkyū* (Studies of the White Lotus Sect in the Ming Period).[d] We await detailed book reviews of it.

Hosoya Yoshio has written two articles on a Daoist group known as the Zhengyi Sect of Longhu Mountain, which reached its zenith in the Yongzheng period of the Qing dynasty. "The Zhengyi Sect of the Yongzheng Reign"[b] (*Tōhōgaku* 72) is concerned particularly with Master Lou Jinyuan; and "The Zhengyi Sect of the Shunzhi and Kangxi Reigns (Part 1)"[c] (*Hirosaki daigaku jimbun gakubu bunkei ronsō* 21.4) introduces the activities of the Zhengyi Sect in these reign periods.

In his essay "The Lineage of the Shouyuan Sect in the Mid-Qing Period"[a] (in *Ran no kōzu*), Usui Takashi describes the lineage of the Shouyuan Sect under Daoist leader Zhang Zaigong, who lived from the late Kangxi era until 1727. Usui shows the links Zhang forged with the religious army of Hubei which touched off the White Lotus Rebellion in the Jiajing period.

On the intellectual characteristics of anti-Christianity in the *Shengchao poxie ji* (Collection of Our August Dynasty on Destroying Heterodoxy), Murayama Naoko has written "On the Anti-Christian Movement at the End of the Ming as Seen in the *Shengchao poxie ji*"[a] (*Ochanomizu shigaku* 29).

Over the past year, some eighty or more books and articles on Ming and Qing history were published, and, owing to space limitations, a fair number of them have not been introduced here. I mention Iwama Kazuo's article "Thought and Society in the Ming"[a] (*Okayama daigaku hōgakkai zasshi* 36.1), which simply explains his own views; but I have been unable to discuss other studies of intellectual history, ethnic minorities, foreign trade, or of the Manchus prior to the invasion of China. Finally, this past year *Higashi Ajia sekai shi tankyū (Examination of the World of East Asian History)*[a] appeared, jointly edited by Teng Weicao, Wang Zhongluo, Okuzaki Yūji, and Kobayashi Kazumi. Although many of the essays in it should have been discussed here, I received the book too late for emendations to the present survey. We look forward to analysis next year.

8

Japanese Studies of Post-Opium War China: 1986

Takeuchi Fusashi, in *Shigaku zasshi*
96.5 (May 1987), 225-232.

Our perspectives on Chinese society are now being rescrutinized. In response to the criticism last year by Kubota Bunji, Mizoguchi Yūzō rebutted with an article, "On the 'Image of Modern China' Again"[c] (*Shichō* n.s. 19), which raises issues in three areas: (1) a fresh look at the accepted hypothesis of the stages of modern Chinese history—from conservatism to early Westernization, to the 1898 Reform Movement, to the 1911 Revolution—which have essentially earned their standards of value from comparison with the modern period in Europe; (2) the need to retrieve an image of modern China as a modern developmental form intrinsic to China based on its own standards of value; and (3) an elucidation of the importance of traditional Chinese thought often represented by views of "feudalism" (*fengjian*). He criticizes the research methodologies which have evaluated various leaders of movements and officials in China on the basis of the extent to which they approach the ultimate standard—the Chinese revolution. There is much worthy of study in Mizoguchi's argument that we need work aimed at finding intrinsic value within Chinese society itself.

   In addition, last year an effort was made by scholars from Japan, China, and Korea to arrive at an understanding of East Asia through a joint venture: the volume *Higashi* (ed. Teng Weicao, Wang Zhongluo, Okuzaki Yūji, and Kobayashi Kazumi). This volume represents a much needed effort to relativize our (Japanese) views of Asia, including China. We look forward to further frank exchanges of views unhindered by national boundaries.

   Efforts to come to terms with Chinese society have tended to advance analysis while accepting a premise of homogeneous social space in China. This is probably due to the fact there has been no differentiation of the elements of modernization theory which placed such value on the homogenization of society and nation-state formation. This image of a homogeneous society in China is treated by Kagami Mitsuyuki in his article "The Cultural Revolution and the Xinjiang Border Area"[a] (in *Gendai Chūgoku no yukue*, *bunka dai kakumei no seisatsu II* [Whither Contemporary China, Reflections on the Cultural Revolution, vol. II]). He points out a similarity in two views which see progress as social homogenization: Chinese notions of ethnicity during the period of the Cultural Revolution when different ethnic groups in China were denied synchronic differences, and the measure of development of an ethnic minority was the degree to which it approached the standard set by Han society; and the conception of modernization in China today which stresses China's "tardiness" to modernize. Kagami states his views on questions of ethnicity quite bluntly. In reexamining this image of society and in adopting a perspective that gives serious consideration to a pluralistic structure, perhaps we should raise issues of ethnicity together with those concerning intermediate social organizations, such as the village, the clan, the guild, and the like. We need also to take another look at problems of concern to individual linguistic social groupings, sections of society, and ethnic minorities, which have been seen as groups that will have to assimilate in the process of nation-state formation.

The Hakkas *(kejia)* belong to a distinct ethnic group in China. Two essays concern the Hakkas: Inada Seiichi, "On the Hakkas at the Time of the Taiping Rebellion"[b] *(Nagoya daigaku Tōyō shi kenkyū hōkoku* 11); and Segawa Masahisa, "Hakka and Punti"[a] *(Minzokugaku kenkyū* 51.2). Inada first notes that the *ke* (or "guest") element of *kejia* (or Hakka, "guest people") in the historical sources does not only refer to the ethnic group known as Hakkas but was also an inclusive designation for immigrant peoples. On this basis he analyzes the reorganization under the community compact *(xiangyue)* and community self-defense *(baojia)* systems[1] in Guiping County, Guangxi Province on the eve of the Taiping Rebellion. The Anliang Compact, formed here on the initiative of gentrymen such as Huang Tizheng in opposition to secret societies of Tiandi (Heaven and Earth) filiation, integrated the various functions of community compact, community self-defense, *tuanlian*, and charity granary systems—all centered around the local native population—and thus gained full control over both native and "guest" peoples. Inada further points out that the heightening of tension between locals and Hakkas was due to the fact that Hakkas—seen as "ruffians" linked to secret societies and objects needing indoctrination—were excluded from the surrounding loci of power. We should note that he does not deal with Hakkas across time and that he tries to clarify their distinct position within their political and social relations.

On the basis of social anthropological fieldwork in rural villages in the New Territories of Hong Kong, Segawa criticizes the work on the Hakkas by Luo Xianglin. He sees them as an ethnic group which has long continued to exist over time and space. He emphasizes that Hakka ethnic groupings live in a state of dependence.

This particular point is treated by Kani Hiroaki in his "On the Boat People of Guangdong under the System of 'Good' and 'Bad' Commoners"[c] (in *Ajia no sabetsu mondai* [Problems of Discrimination in Asia].[c] In this fascinating essay, Kani points out the peculiarities of these people (*danhu*), who lived on boats in south China. They were looked down upon and were hostile to state authority and the social order. He notes that these groups of boat people had not existed as such from time immemorial and had taken form socially as a result of external conditions.

The Chūgoku jōkyo kenkyū gurūpu (Study Group on Chinese Dwellings, Tokyo Geijutsu University) published a report entitled "Chinese Homes and Hakka Dwellings"[a] (*Jūtaku kenchiku* 144). This detailed research report concerns Hakka dwellings in Yongding and Nanjing Counties, Fujian Province, and helps us understand how Hakkas have lived in the modern era.

"Minority peoples" in south China include ethnic groups other than Hakkas. Tsukada Shigeyuki's article, "A Study of the Zhuang People Becoming Tenant Farmers in the Ming and Qing Eras"[a] (*Tōyō gakuhō* 67.1-2), is essential to any understanding of the Zhuang. He argues that the process through which Zhuang became tenant farmers began in the early Ming with the proffering of land reclamation labor power and armed might for Han landlords; in the Qing, the Zhuang's distinctive social system began to dissolve and take on Han characteristics. As Tsukada notes, we need a study of the survival of Zhuang under the aboriginal office (*tusi*) and those not under it, as well as a concrete examination of the formation of local Han society which set the parameters for the Zhuang. If, as argued here, ethnicity takes shape in relation to political and social conditions, then the organization and integration of various groupings in Chinese society are issues of concern.

Hamashita Takeshi deals with this problem in his essay, "The Tribute Trade System and Modern Asia"[g] (*Kokusai seiji* 8). He suggests the concept of a "tribute trade system" as the internal cohesive glue within Asia, for, in his view developed over the years, Asian history must be understood as "a historical entity with organic bonds." He offers two characteristics for such a system. First, bearing tribute took systemic form through the expansion outward of the principle of domestic control (including heterogeneous ethnic elements); enveloping social groups at a variety of levels—from the center to the provinces, to border areas (officials in aboriginal areas), to tribute-bearing states, to trading states; and giving structure to an organic system that integrated the center with the periphery. Second, tribute relations were not merely conceptual; they formed a network for trade, and within this framework gave form to a unified sphere for the liquidation of silver accounts. He argues that, in the development of modern Asian and Sino-Japanese relations, as Japan faced modernization, it assumed the tasks, politically, of reorganizing Sino-Japanese-Ryukyuan-Korean relations, and, economically, of overcoming the monopoly of control in commercial relations—namely, tribute trade—held by the Central Kingdom. Hamashita offers a fresh perspective on the tribute system, which has been used as an analytic concept for foreign relations, by including areas which need be treated within the analytic structure of the state. We look forward to further research on the development of the system itself.

I would like now to turn to individual studies in rough chronological order. In his article "An Analysis of Issues in Coastal Defense at the Time of the First Opium War"[a] (*Gifu daigaku kyōiku gakubu kenkyū hōkoku—jimbun kagaku* 34), Fujita Keiichi argues that the awareness among the "people" (*min*) of a foreign war did not exist; that "officials" (*guan*) lacked a territorial sense of responsibility; and that, furthermore, no awareness of integration between the "people" and the "state" existed in this period.

Nagano Shin'ichirō's essay, "England's Policy Concerning the Taipings (Part 1)"[b] (*Daidō bunka daigaku Tōyō kenkyū* 78), examines Great Britain's Taiping policy from the signing of the Tianjin Treaty through the Beijing Agreement. He traces the process as the British shifted from neutrality to military intervention.

In his piece "The Coolie Trade and the Incident of the Ship Robert Baun"[b] (*Ryūkyū daigaku kyōiku gakubu kiyō* 29), Nishizato Yoshiyuki places this incident—a rebellion of coolies in 1852 in the midst of the growing "coolie trade"—in the international context of East Asia, including Ryukyuan-Chinese relations at the time. We await more detailed research.

Itō Teruo, in his "A Study of the Sino-French War and East Asia"[a] (*Yokohama shiritsu daigaku ronsō—jimbun kagaku keiretsu* 37.2-3), examines views on the Sino-French War held by Japanese at the time. He places them within the context of bonds forged by Japan, Korea, the Ryukyus, and Taiwan with the Qing government.

Nakada Yoshinobu's article, "From 'Traitor' to 'Patriot'"[b] (*Shūjitsu joshi daigaku shigaku ronshū* 1), examines in detail the issues involved in contemporary Chinese evaluations of Zuo Zongtang, who was abruptly "rehabilitated" in recent Chinese scholarship on the early Westernizers. Nakada casts serious doubt on the prevailing Chinese view that regards Zuo's defeat of Yakub Beg as a contribution to the unification of China.

Fuma Susumu's essay, "The Management of Foundling Homes and Local Society in Songjiang"[c] (*Tōyōshi kenkyū* 45.3), introduces in great detail the organization and management of homes for foundlings in Songjiang, a system spread across a number of cities for the care of homeless infants. He clarifies how voluntary management through popular donations and land revenues accompanied the increase in the number of foundlings and eventually compelled reliance on the state and local officials.

A number of articles deal with the reorganization of local control in Jiangnan following the Taiping Rebellion: Natsui Haruki, "On the Problem of Immigrants in Western Zhejiang after the Taiping Rebellion"[c] (*Chikaki ni arite* 9); Natsui Haruki, "On Landlord-Tenant Relations in Suzhou in the Late Qing"[d] (*Hokkaidō kyōiku daigaku kiyō—shakai kagaku hen* 36.1); Kishimoto Mio, "The Conception of Landownership in the *Zuhe*"[a] (*Chūgoku—shakai to bunka* 1); and Usui Sachiko, "On Tax Reforms in Jiangsu Province in 1865"[b] (*Tōyō shi kenkyū* 45.2).

Natsui's first essay analyzes immigration policy concerning "guest people" *(kemin)* which aimed at reviving agricultural production, securing financial revenues, and (following the dissolution of the Hunan Army) returning the troops to the land. He also looks at the influences exerted by immigrants on Zhejiang society. His second essay describes in great detail the *Xianfeng Tongzhi nian zuce* (Annual Rent Registers for the Xiangfeng and Tongzhi Reigns), held in the library of Hitotsubashi University. On the basis of his analysis, he shows that the rent reduction implemented by the local gentry in Suzhou in 1865 (Tongzhi 4) brought about an equalization of tenancy conditions. He also infers, as a cause for this reduction, the development of a rent resistance movement and an increase in resident landlords.

Kishimoto's article argues that, according to Tao Xu's logic, the one-field two-owners system was a common bond through joint investment of landlord and tenant. For the "mutual benefit" of both sides, Tao sought a rent reduction. She points out that Tao's reasoning ignored the fact that the high cost of topsoil rights in Suzhou in the late Qing originated in the "small farmer mentality" of tenants who gave the greatest priority to the stability and security of "wages" while they suffered insufficienct cultivation opportunities. The effort to elucidate the economic logic of tenant farmers who persisted in the maintenance of such topsoil rights is extremely suggestive as well in trying to understand peasant activities in popular movements. Also useful in this area is the book by Huang Zongzhi [Philip Huang] *Huabei xiaonong jingji yu shehui bianqian* (The Small Peasant Economy of North China and Social Change),[a] which sheds light on the small peasant ethos to which the avoidance of danger (i.e., safety first) was elemental and diametrically opposed to the utilitarian economic activity of manager-landlords in North China.

Usui's article examines the tax reforms implemented in 1865 in the Suzhou area. She demonstrates that Suzhou gentrymen, such as Feng Guifen, who sought a reduction in such things as tribute rice to the center and the levying of taxes under gentry guidance, were frustrated by the pressure of local officials who gave first priority to stabilizing central government finances. She also points up the relationship between the gentry *(shenshi)* of that time and local officials, between the center and the locality.

On the early Westernization *(yangwu)* and reform movements, we have an essay by Meguro Katsuhiko, "The Historical Position of the Bureau of Protection and Defense (Baoweiju) in the Hunan Reform Movement"[c] (*Tōhoku daigaku Tōyō shi ronshū* 2). He offers a positive evaluation of the

Bureau of Protection and Defense instituted by such Hunanese reformers as Huang Zunxian and Chen Baozhen. These were men, he argues, who avoided conflict with the Western powers and aimed at social stability and commercial and industrial development for Hunan. He also stresses the qualitative difference between these reformist policies and those of conservative officials. Fukazawa Hideo has written a piece on the academies which were set up in the period of the reform movement: "The Canxueguan of Hangzhou (Zhejiang) and the Reform Movement"[d] (*Arutesu riberaresu* 39).

Ōtani Toshio published two essays: "An Examination of Statecraft Thought in the Period of the Early Westernization Movement"[g] (*Kadai shigaku* 33); and "The Present State and Future Tasks in the Study of Lin Zexu"[h] (*Kagoshima daigaku hōbungakubu kiyō—jimbun kagaku ronshū* 24). The first of these calls for a reevaluation of the perspective that has simply seen the policies of *yangwu* officials as reactionary. The latter piece introduces directions in recent research on Lin Zexu in China and Japan.

On the political structure of the late Qing, we have an article by Mizoguchi Yūzō, "Views on the Parliamentary System in the Early Guangxu Period"[c] (*Kagoshima daigaku hōbungakubu kiyō—jimbun kagaku ronshū* 24). He examines the background to Zhang Shusheng's 1884 memorial on the introduction of a parliamentary system. He shows that interest among *yangwu* officials at the time for Western institutions, such as the parliamentary system, was definitely becoming widespread.

In the first part of a longer essay, "The Development of Republican Thought in China and the Circumstances Surrounding the Taiwan Democratic Independence Movement"[c] (*Kindai Chūgoku* 18), Sasaki Masaya examines in great detail how Chinese intellectuals, such as Wei Yuan, Liang Tingnan, and Jiang Dunfu, understood and explained the American republican and constitutional systems.

Mitsuishi Zenkichi's article, "Cliques and Political Parties"[b] (*Chūgoku—Shakai to bunka* 1), offers a reevaluation of late Qing political thought. Abjuring the names ordinarily used—the *yangwu* clique, the reformist clique, the conservative clique, and the like—he sets up as his analytic coordinates the formation of political parties from traditionalism, enlightened traditionalism, modern conservatism, and Confucian factional politics, through study societies and pressure groups, to modern conservatism and conservative political parties.

In "Views on Local Autonomy in the Late Qing"[b] (*Chiiki bunka kenkyū* 11), Kusunose Masaaki examines the circumstances surrounding the switch in position by constitutional reformers, before the establishment of provincial assemblies, from a priority for local autonomy to a call for the rapid convening of a national assembly.

Nakagawa Yasuko's article, "The New Regime in Zhili in the Late Qing"[b] (*Shisō** 27), looks at the policies of Chen Xiongfan, Magistrate of Miyun County, Shuntian Prefecture, Zhili. Chen stressed local civil control in the *baojia* system, educational institutions, and encouragement to agriculture. Nakagawa shows what actually transpired in the implementation of a new local regime at the county level during the Guangxu reign.

Research on the 1911 Revolution reflects the depth of academic ties with the People's Republic of China in recent years. The publication in Japanese of two volumes, which deserve separate reviews, are evidence of this point: *Son Chūzan kenkyū Nit-Chū kokusai gakujutsu tōronkai hōkokushū* (Papers from the Sino-Japanese International Symposium for Studies of Sun Zhong-shan,[a] ed. Son Bun kenkyūkai [Society for Sun Studies]); and Hu Sheng, et al., *Shingai kakumei* (The 1911 Revolution).[a] Let me now turn to individual articles in this area.

First, Kubota Bunji's article, "Was the 1911 Revolution an Absolutist Transformation?"[d] (in *Higashi*), offers a critique of Yokoyama Suguru's view that the 1911 Revolution embodied China's transition to absolutism. Kubota criticizes Yokoyama for taking the bourgeois revolutions in modern Europe (with China unable to complete the anti-imperialist, anti-colonialist course) to stipulate "absolutism," idealizing that revolutionary process, and then stressing the incomplete quality of China's "revolution" with this as a standard.

In his essay "The 1911 Revolution in Guangdong"[a] (*Kokushikan daigaku bungakubu jimbun gakkai kiyō* 18), Maeda Shōtarō traces the political process from the establishment of a regime in Guangdong through the failure of the second revolution against Yuan Shikai. He locates the reasons for this failure in the political alienation of the people and the army who stood for the revolutionaries' compromise with the constitutionalists and for popular interests.

Hazama Naoki, in his "Democracy and Autocracy in the Thought of Sun Zhongshan"[a] (*Tōhō gakuhō* 58), examines the inclinations toward autocracy and submissiveness inherent in Sun Zhongshan's ideas at the time of his rivalry with Huang Xing over the organization principles for the Chinese Revolutionary Party (Zhonghua gemingdang).

Gotō Nobuko published one segment of a longer piece in progress: "Zhang Shizhao in the Era of the *Minlibao*"[a] (*Shinshū daigaku jimbun gakubu jimbun kagaku ronshū* 20). She discusses in this segment the views of Zhang Shizhao, editor-in-chief of *Minlibao*, on a responsible cabinet system of government at the time of the Lu Zhengxiang Cabinet, and she considers the criticisms expressed by Wu Zhihui and Zai Tianchou of Zhang's views.

Yokoyama Hiroaki's article, "The Republican Revolutionary Movement in China and Secret Societies"[a] (*Meiji gakuin daigaku hōgaku kenkyū* 37), examines the political significance of the fact that the revolutionary movement, based on the Western republican ideas of Sun Zhongshan, was carried out by a traditional secret society.

Kojima Yoshio's essay, "On the Chinese National Assembly (Part 5)"[a]

(*Shingai kakumei kenkyū* 6), follows chronologically from Yokoyama's. He traces the activities in Shanghai and elsewhere of the Chinese National Assembly. Mitsushima Toku deals with Sino-Tibetan relations during the period before and after the 1911 Revolution, in his article "On Uprisings in Tibet at the End of the Qing and Early in the Republic"[b] (*Kokushikan daigaku kyōyō ronshū* 22).

In her essay "On the Birth of Patriotic Cotton Cloth"[a] (*Kōbe daigaku shigaku nempō* 1), Rinbara Fumiko shows that patriotic cotton cloth (*aiguobu*), which later became the symbol of the anti-Japanese boycott movement, was initially produced at the time of the anti-American boycott movement of 1905 by Song Zejiu of Tianjin.

Mori Tokihiko, in "The Modernization of China and Overseas Students"[a] (*Aichi daigaku kokusai mondai kenkyūjo kiyō* 81), looks at Li Shizeng, the originator of the work-study program in France. He considers the roles played by overseas students in modern China.

The *Sanshi nian riji* (Diary of Thirty Years) of Huang Zunsan, who left Hunan to study in Japan in 1905, was translated by Sanetō Keishū and Satō Saburō: *Shinkokujin Nihon ryūgaku nikki* (Diary of a Chinese Student in Japan).[a] This is an invaluable document for understanding the activities of overseas Chinese student society in Japan at that time.

In addition, Katayama Hyōe's essay, "On the Education of the Princely Establishment (*wangfu*) of Inner Mongolia in the Late Qing"[a] (in *Nakamura*), discusses the educational activities of Japanese in the late Qing.

We move now to essays on social and economic history. Sugiyama Nobuya's article, "The Structure of 'Foreign Pressure' in East Asia"[a] (*Rekishigaku kenkyū* 560), is a masterpiece that points out the disparity between the image and the reality of "foreign pressure" in 19th century East Asia. This breaks down into two principal points. First, the military might of Great Britain in East Asia from 1860 through the middle of the 1880's did not go beyond the defense of concession areas because of a policy of reducing military expenditures and personnel, for Britain lacked the conditions necessary for long-term colonial control. Thus, second, the primary form which trade in East Asia assumed over the latter half of the 19th century was concession trade. Meanwhile, Western capital was excluded from the structure of circulation, because the Chinese commercial and circulatory mechanisms were linked to the Chinese systems of guilds or sales and claims. It played no direct role in domestic markets; on the contrary, he argues, Western capital encouraged the establishment of an independent economic system—that is, a commercial and circulation structure—within East Asia.

Miyata Michiaki's masterful article, "Market Structure along the Chinese Coast in the Latter Half of the 19th Century"[a] (*Rekishigaku kenkyū* 550), stresses the force exerted by "foreign pressure" on the mechanisms of circulation in Asian societies. He demonstrates that market circulation for the transportation of such commodities as soybean waste, raw cotton, and sugar through the late 19th century was both expansive and stable. In particular, he shows that, despite the advance of foreign ships into domestic sea lanes following the opening of Chinese ports, Chinese merchant ships and commodity circulation continued as in the past. Within the domestic market structure of China, Miyata also examines the resistance of domestic commercial products to the intrusion of capitalist products.

In "The Social Response to the Modern Silk Industry"[a] (in *Sanshigyō*), Furuta Kazuko reports on the symposium on Chinese sericulture held last year. From the perspective of social structure, she compares the cases of the Jōshū area in Japan and Huzhou in China as each responded to the modern sericulture industry. Whereas in the Chinese case, she argues, village communalism entered into the introduction and spread of new technologies and in cooperative consignment, in Japan one finds the independence of business dealers, namely individual farmers, negotiating advance brokering in market towns in the buying and selling of manufactured goods.

Suzuki Tomoo's essay, "The Expansion of the Raw Silk Trade in Shanghai in the Era of Early Westernization"[g] (in *Sanshigyō*), deals with the period from the middle through the late 19th century. He argues that "Jiang-Zhe silk," which held a dominant position in European markets, lost its ascendancy by virtue of the revival of European silk thread in the early 1870's, the lowering of quality of "Jiang-Zhe silk," and illegal transactions by "silk dealers." Native sericulture in Jiangsu and Zhejiang and the raw silk trade in Shanghai then faced a crisis.

Nakai Hideki's work, "The Management of a Limited Liability Company in the Late Qing and Early Republican Periods"[a] (in *Henkakki*), looks at the Dasheng Cotton Mill in Nantong, which had succeeded exceptionally well in enterprises set up by Zhang Jian late in the Qing era but was unable to transform itself into a modern commercial structure and thus fell apart. He blames its failure on poor business management and the deficient leadership capacities of the government.

In his essay "The 1911 Revolution and Japan's Response"[a] (*Shingai kakumei kenkyū* 6), Li Tingjiang clarifies the fact that the establishment of the Central Bank of China, as a means to secure the currency reform and gold standard, was proposed by Sakatani Yoshirō after the Russo-Japanese War.

Tsukase Susumu's article, "On Problems in Joint Sino-Japanese Management of the Hanyeping Company during the Period of the 1911 Revolution"[a] (*Chūō daigaku daigakuin ronkyū—bungaku kenkyū kahen* 18.1), describes in detail how the Japanese plans for a joint Sino-Japanese management of the Hanyeping Company took advantage of the chaos in the revolutionary period and the fiscal pressures at work on the revolutionary regime.

He traces the process by which these plans dissolved as Sun Zhongshan resigned as provisional president and a fierce resistance to plans for joint management was launched by the constitutionalists and the Hubei military government.

Kada Hirokazu, in his essay "The China Merchant Steamship Company and the Nanjing Provisional Government"[a] (*Hiroshima daigaku Tōyō shi kenkyūshitsu hōkoku* 8), examines the response of the China Merchant Steamship Company (and the factional strife within it), which had grown by virtue of its reliance on the power of the Qing court, to the turmoil of the 1911 Revolution period. He looks at the issues surrounding the loans taken by the Nanjing provisional government from Japan to measure this response.

Nakamura Tadashi's article, "Views on the Late Qing Monetary System"[e] (*Nihon daigaku keizai gakubu keizai kagaku kenkyūjo kiyō* 10), argues that, during the disorder in the Hunan provincial fiscal administration in the Xuantong reign and after, the Hunan monetary bureau, which replaced the Funan monetary bureau set up during the reform movement in Hunan, expanded the amount of currency issued. This led to further currency chaos.

Kuroda Akinobu, in his "The Circulation of Currency in the Middle and Lower Yangzi Delta in the Early 20th Century"[c] (in *Nihon ryōjikan hōkoku no kenkyū* [Studies of Japanese Consular Reports],[a] ed. Tsunoyama Sakae), offers a different perspective. In the late 19th century, local functional specialization in the circulation of currency—namely, silver in the coastal areas and copper in the hinterland—collapsed in conjunction with the unification of the silver *yuan* by Yuan Shikai in the decade of the 1910's and the spread of tender from the Bank of China which accompanied this unification. Kuroda investigates in great detail the process by which currency unification in both areas (coastal and inland) and their mutual relationship were strengthened. He concludes that the groundwork was taking shape for the introduction of a system of supervised currency even in areas where the political situation was warlord chaos.

Studies concerned with popular movements were few in number last year, and the strenuous efforts of scholars from China were remarkable. Let us look first at work on the period of the Taiping Rebellion. Wang Qingcheng's article, "The *Tianfu shengzhi*, the *Tianxiong shengshu*, and the History of the Taiping Rebellion"[a] (2 parts, *Rōhyakushō no sekai* 3, 4), is an extremely detailed introduction to the historical texts known as *Tianfu shengzhi* and *Tianxiong shengshu* (records left by Yang Xiuqing and Xiao Chaogui, recently discovered in England). Wang offers some important source material for research on the early Taiping movement which were hitherto completely unknown.

Namiki Yorihisa's essay, "North China at the Time of the Taiping Rebellion (Part 1)"[c] (*Tōkai daigaku bungakubu kiyō* 44), presents biographies of Nian rebel leaders, Zhang Luoxing and others, by using the fieldwork and songs compiled by Mr. Jiang Di.

In their article "The Activities of Boats on Lake Chao along the Lower Reaches of the Yangzi in the Late Qing"[b] (*Fukuoka joshi tandai kiyō* 30), Fukuda Setsuo and Tsutsumi Kazuyuki trace the activities of boats on Lake Chao from the Taiping period through the years of the Guangxu reign.

Sasaki Masaya's essay, "Notices of Anti-Christian Rumors in Guangdong, Fujian, and Hunan Localities in 1871"[d] (*Kindai Chūgoku* 18), introduces from British Foreign Office documents notices concerning the anti-Christian movement which spread to various locales on the basis of rumors about the scattering of a magical dust from Foshan in Guangdong.

Kobayashi Kazumi has published a volume entitled *Giwadan sensō to Meiji kokka* (The Boxer War and the Meiji State).[c] This is a major work which, in addition to gathering together Kobayashi's studies of the Boxers over the past years, sheds light on the military intervention of the Meiji government. We look forward to detailed reviews by the appropriate reviewers.

Shimamoto Nobuko, in her article "The White Wolf Uprising (Part 1)"[a] (*Rōhyakushō no sekai* 4), deals with the formaton of White Wolf's group and its early activities around the time of the 1911 Revolution.

In "The Implementation of the Examination of Land Deeds in North Chinese Villages in the Early Republican Period and Popular Movements"[b] (*Shundai shigaku* 66), Uchiyama Masao examines the relationship between peasants in North China and state power through a case involving the murder of the Leyun County magistrate (Shandong Province). The magistrate, currying favor from the Beiyang warlord regime after the founding of the Republic of China, had tried to enforce a new tax on the examination of land deeds.

Finally, I would like to look at a few articles that deal with intellectual history. Two pieces concern the Buddhist thinker Yang Wenhui who exerted an enormous influence on late Qing reformers: Fujitani Kōetsu, "Yang Wenhui's Career and His View of Society"[c] (in *Ran no kōzu*); and Lou Yulie, "A Promoter of Modern Chinese Buddhism"[a] (*Tōyō gakujutsu kenkyū* 25.1). Fujitani diligently traces Yang's contacts with the reformers of the 1898 period and his social activities, and he examines Yang's conception of society. Lou discusses in great detail Yang's Buddhist ideas, which were based on his own conception of Pure Land thought, laying emphasis both on accomplishment through one's own capacities and through those of the Buddha.

We have two essays on Liang Qichao. Abe Ken'ichi's "One Aspect of Liang Qichao's Enlightenment Activities"[b] (*Ran no kōzu*) discusses Liang's activities as a reformer promoting such things as language reform. In his essay "Late Qing Nationalism and the Theory of the Organic Nature of the State"[b] (*Hiroshima daigaku bungakubu kiyō* 45), Yokoyama Suguru examines Liang Qichao's theory of the state from the era of the 1898 Reform Movement through the 1911 Revolution. He focuses attention on Liang's notion of the state as an organic entity.

Tang Zhijun's articles on Kang Youwei and Zhang Binglin have now been translated by Shino Michiko: *Kindai Chūgoku no kakumei shisō to Nihon* (Modern Chinese Revolutionary Thought and Japan).[b] Reviews of this volume should be left to specialized reviewers.

Sakamoto Hiroko's article, "Zhang Binglin's Idea of the Individual and Consciousness-Only Buddhism"[b] (*Shisō* 747), ranges over the thought and activities of Zhang Binglin after the 1911 Revolution. She looks at the formation of his later conception that all things were of one essence, which was clearly of a different sort from that of traditional Chinese ideas along these lines. Through his encounter with consciousness-only Buddhism, Zhang had developed his ideas on racial differentiation and stress on the individual.

In recent years, a number of articles—such as Ishida Hiroshi's "An Analysis of the Structural Transformation of the Rural Chinese Society and Economy"[a] (*Kansai daigaku keizai ronshū* 35.5, 36.1) and Ueda Makoto's "How Cohesive Forces Function in the Village"[c] (*Chūgoku kenkyū geppō* 455, 456)—are the results of fieldwork in China. As such research becomes more systematic, a more three-dimensional picture of Chinese society should emerge. Contracts and other kinds of documents which still remain among the populace are excellent materials for social historical research. Hamashita Takeshi and others have recently edited and published a catalogue to documents (held in the Tōyō bunka kenkyūjo at Tokyo University) concerning the buying and selling of land and homes, covering the period from the Qing through the Republic: *Tōyō bunka kenkyūjo shozai Chūgoku tochi bunsho mokuroku, kaisetsu* (Catalogue to the Chinese Land Documents Held in the Tōyō bunka kenkyūjo, with an Expanation).[h]

Notes

(All notes are those of the translator unless otherwise indicated).

Chapter 1

1. See the two essays by Katayama Tsuyoshi: "The *Tujia biao* and Problems Surrounding It for the Pearl River Delta of Guangdong in the Late Qing"[a] (*Shigaku zasshi* 91.4); and "On the *Tujia* System in the Pearl River Delta of Guangdong During the Qing Dynasty"[b] (*Tōyō gakuhō* 63.3-4).

2. Mori Masao proposed the new-old concept of *chiiki shakai* in a series of publications over the past several years, most clearly in a piece discussed in my summary of last year's work on the Ming-Qing period by Japanese scholars. See *Ch'ing-shih wen-t'i* 5.1 (June 1984), pp. 83-85; or Joshua A. Fogel, *Recent Japanese Studies of Modern Chinese History*, Armonk, M. E. Sharpe, Inc., Publisher, 1984, pp. 140-41.

3. *Zongguan* was an enshrined deity, the object of religious ritual, probably dating to a military official who managed the transport of tax monies to the North in the late Yuan dynasty. The practice spread of enshrining the local "governors" (a rough translation of *zongguan*) to whom temples remain but whose names are now lost. See the Hamashima essay in question, and E. T. C. Werner, *A Dictionary of Chinese Mythology*, Shanghai, Kelley & Walsh, 1932, pp. 524-25.

4. "Tax captains," in Ray Huang's translation. See his *Taxation and Governmental Finance in Sixteenth-Century Ming China*, Cambridge, Cambridge University Press, p. 36.

5. See Hoshi Ayao, *Chūgoku shakai keizai shi goi* (Vocabulary for Chinese Social and Economic History),[b] pp. 129-30.

6. See Hoshi[b], p. 19. See also R. Bin Wong, "Food Riots in the Qing Dynasty," *Journal of Asian Studies* XLI.4 (August 1982), pp. 767-88.

7. See Hoshi[b], p. 153.

8. On the concept of "reproduction" (*saiseisan*) in Japanese Sinology, see *Ch'ing-shih wen-t'i* 4.9 (June 1983), p. 74; or Fogel, pp. 180-81. See also *State and Society in China: Japanese Perspectives on Ming-Qing Social and Economic History*, ed. Linda Grove and Christian Daniels, Tokyo, University of Tokyo Press, 1984, pp. 245-46.

Chapter 2

1. For a discussion of the Fujii-Kusano debate at considerable length and detail, see Fogel, pp. 58-66.
2. See *ibid.*, pp. 158, 160 for a discussion of part 1 of this essay.

Chapter 3

1. This was a kind of slash and burn method used in early Chinese agriculture to make the soil more fertile. Hoshi[b],p. 29.
2. Hoshi[b], p. 243.
3. Author's note. The first of these two articles examines the dual nature of the Qing as a conquest dynasty and as a Chinese dynasty, because the political change in Chinese history which we are apt to see as a unified dynasty of Han Chinese must also been seen from the perspective of a period of fragmentation and an alien dynasty. The author searches for its origins in the period of the establishment of the "Great Qing" prior to the conquest of China, and he points out that in the process of establishing both civil and military visages the Qing was forming a state of ethnic complexity. The second essay continues the first and treats the formation of a China with five major ethnic groups (lasting till today). Ishibashi looks at periods that prefigured this phenomenon in the Liao, Song, and Jin, and argues that the process was completed under the unified dynasties of Yuan, Ming, and Qing. Thus, he points out, "the economic development of Jiangnan and the growth of a political center around Beijing were decisive and heightened the level of dependence on a political center in the capital area of Beijing and a rice-cultivating center in Jiangnan, particularly along the lower reaches of the Yangzi River. This invited an excessive tax burden on the peasantry. Furthermore, the distancing of the political center in the North from the economic center in the South proved indispensible to the development of the Grand Canal and the establishment of the Grain Tribute System" (p. 19). Among the social changes that occurred in conjunction with this, we see changes in production relations in the Zhejiang region whereby auxiliary handicraft labor became one principal form of work, a shift of the central rice growing region to Hubei and Hunan, and the rise of social discontent concerning labor power in the grain tribute system.
4. Charles O. Hucker, *A Dictionary of Official Titles in Imperial China*, Stanford, Stanford University Press, 1985, col. 157.
5. In the Ming, these were personal attendants attached to palace eunuchs; in the Qing, they were personal servants of high provincial and prefectural officials. Hucker, col. 116; Hoshi[b], p. 290.
6. See Fogel, p. 117, for an analysis of this section when it appeared as an article.

7. Thanks to Christian Daniels of Shūjitsu Women's College for helping me decipher this and several other technical points in this translation.

8. This is the collection compiled in the 1930's by interviewers and scholars employed by the Research Department of the South Manchurian Railway Company.

Chapter 4

1. *Juhua* were poor women sold into effective slavery in Guangdong to serve as prostitutes overseas in the United States and Europe: *ju* 'pig' (as in pig tail) and *hua* 'flower' (in Cantonese this term carries the implication of depravity or prostitution). See Kani's major work *Kindai Chūgoku no kūri to "choka"* (Coolies and "juhua" in China). For discussion of this book see Fogel, pp. 51, 177-78.

2. This point in the text concludes Usui's portion, and the rest of the piece was written by Kurihara.

Chapter 6

1. Tokunaga Shōjirō, *Kawase to Shinyō, kokusai kessai seido no shi teki tenkai* (Exchange and Trust: The Historical Development of the International Settlement System)[a]; and Hamashita Takeshi, "A Study of the Trade Circulation in Modern China,"[d] *Tōyō gakuhō* 57. 3-4 (March 1976).

2. Hamashita Takeshi, "Asia and the Formation of the Capitalist, Colonialist System,"[e] in *Kōza Chūgoku kin-gendai shi* (Essays on the Modern and Contemporary History of China).

3. William T. Rowe, *Hankow: Commerce and Society in a Chinese City, 1796-1889*, Stanford University Press, 1984. For a study of Shanghai limited to the export trade system, see Motono Eiichi, "The Traffic Revolution: Remaking the Export Sales System in China, 1860-1875," *Modern China* 12.1 (January 1986), pp. 75-102.

4. Author's note. *The North-China Herald*, 17 February 1876, pp. 134-35; and *The Economist*, 11 March 1876, pp. 311-12.

5. Motono's portion of this essay ends with this paragraph, and the rest of the piece was written by Sakamoto.

Chapter 7

1. Shiga is here responding to Terada[a] and Terada.[b] A fuller analysis of the debate between Fujii Hiroshi and Kusano Yasushi, to which Terada was responding, can be found in Fogel, pp. 59-66. The debate includes a divergence of opinion concerning the terms *chengjia, maijia, guotou*, and *dingshou*.

2. See Fogel, pp. 63-64 for an explanation.

3. See Fogel, pp, 64-65 for more information.

4. Translation of this and subsequent terms—Metropolitan Graduate, Provincial Graduate, National University Student, and Clerical Official, respectively—are described in Hucker, col. 167, 197, 150, 308, respectively.

5. See Hoshi Ayao,[b] p. 74.

6. A system whereby every five years a census would be carried out and the population figures entered on the household registers. See *Shinjigen*, comp. Ogawa Tamaki, Nishida Taichirō, and Akatsuka Kiyoshi, p. 786.

7. *Beidonggu* was a system established in 1759 for the authorities in Guangxi to store 100,000 *dan* of rice.

8. "In Ming times, *sheren* [or houseman] was a salaried but unranked status for younger brothers, sons, cousins, and unrelated hangers-on of hereditary military officers, from among whom vacancies in the officer corps were commonly filled." Hucker, col. 417.

9. See Kawagoe's earlier work on the *weixuanfu*: "On the Appointment to Provincial Military Posts of Guard and Battalion (*weiso*) Officials in the Ming: The *Weixuanfu*" (*Chūō daigaku bungakubu kiyō* 24), discussed in Fogel, p. 34.

Chapter 8

1. Translations of bureaucratic and institutional terminology follow Hucker.

Reigns of the Ming and Qing Dynasties

MING		QING	
Emperor	*Year of Accession*	*Emperor*	*Year of Accession*
Hongwu	1368	Shunzhi	1644
Jianwen	1399	Kangxi	1662
Yongle	1403	Yongzheng	1723
Hongxi	1425	Qianlong	1736
Xuande	1426	Jiaqing	1796
Zhengtong	1436	Daoguang	1821
Jingtai	1450	Xianfeng	1851
Tianshun	1457	Tongzhi	1862
Chenghua	1465	Guangxu	1875
Hongzhi	1488	Xuantong	1908
Zhengde	1506		
Jiajing	1522		
Longqing	1567		
Wanli	1573		
Taichang	1620		
Tianqi	1621		
Chongzhen	1628		

Articles and Books Cited
(Alphabetically by Author)

ABE Hiroshi 阿部洋
a. 清末における学堂教育と日本人教習：直隷省の場合

ABE Ken'ichi 阿部賢一
a. 鄒容の「革命軍」と西洋近代思想：「民約論」と進化論とを中心に
b. 梁啓超の啓蒙活動の一端について

ADACHI Keiji 足立啓二
a. 中国前近代史研究と封建制
b. 清～民国期における農業経営の発展
c. 中国封建制論の批判的検討
d. 清代蘇州府下における地主的土地所有の展開

AJIOKA Tōru 味岡徹
a. 袁世凱政府財政の破綻と兌換停止令
b. 護国戦争後の地方自治回復：江蘇省を中心に
c. ロシア革命後の東三省北部における「幣権回収」

ARAKI Kengo 荒木見悟
a. 陽明学の開展と仏教 (Tokyo, Kenbun shuppan, 1984).

ARITA Kazuo 有田和夫
a. 清末意識構造の研究 (Tokyo, Kyūko shoin, 1984).

ASAI Motoi 浅井紀
a. 明清宗教結社と民衆
b. 清代青蓮教の道統について

BANNO Masataka 坂野正高
a. 中国近代化と馬建忠　(Tokyo, Tokyo University Press, 1985).

BASTID-BRUGIÈRE, Marianne (trans. SHIMADA Kenji 島田虔次　　and
　HASE Etsuhiro 長部悦弘)
a. 清末のヨーロッパへの留学生たち

BEPPU Sunao 別府淳夫
a. 康有為と荀子
b. 梁啓超における西洋と伝統

CHEN Jian 陳建
a. 中国歴史学界における洋務運動研究の新動向

CHEN Zhengti 陳正是
a. 台湾における「中国意議」と「台湾意識」：最近の文学・思想
　界での論争を中心に

CHŪGOKU jōkyo kenkyū gurūpu 中国城居石研究グループ
a. 中国民居・客家のすまい

CHŪGOKU shi kenkyūkai 中国史研究会
a. 中国史像の再構成：国家と農民 (Tokyo, Bunrikaku, 1983).

DAI Guohui 戴国煇
a. 中国廿蔗糖業の展開 (Tokyo, Ajia keizai kenkyūjo, 1967).

DANIELS, Christian
a. 清末台湾南部製糖業と商人資本：一八七〇～
   一八九五年
b. 清代台湾南部における製糖業の構造：とくに一八六〇
   年以前を中心として
c. 中国砂糖の国際的位置

DANJŌ Hiroshi 檀上寛
a. 「鄭氏規範」の世界：明朝権力と富民層
b. 方孝孺の政治思想：明初の理想的君主観
c. 明代科挙改革の政治的背景

DING Richu 丁日初
a. 中国近代経済史研究の状況

DING Richu and DU Xuncheng 杜恂誠 (trans. IKEDA Makoto 池田
誠 , et al)
a. 一九世紀中国・日本における資本主義的近代化の成否の原因に
関する初歩的分析

EBITANI Naonori 海老谷尚典
a. 章炳麟における種族主義の形成：戊戌以後，蘇報案に
かけての理論

ENATSU Yoshiki 江夏由樹
a. 清末の時期，東三省南部における官地の丈放の社会経済
的意味：錦州官荘の丈放を一例として

ENOKI Kazuo 榎一雄
a. 新疆の建省：二十世紀の中央アジア
b. 明代のマカオ

FUJII Hiroshi 藤井宏
a. 一田両主制の基本構造
b. 初期一田両主制の新研究

FUJII Shōzō 藤井昇三
a. 旧海軍省編纂の辛亥革命関係資料について

FUJII Tomoko 藤井友子
a. 唐才常の「通」について

FUJIOKA Kikuo　藤岡喜久男
a. 張謇と東南互保
b. 張謇と辛亥革命　(Sapporo, Hokudai tosho kankōkai, 1985).

FUJITA Keiichi　藤田敬一
a. 第一次アヘン戦争期における海防問題試論

FUJITANI Kōetsu　藤谷浩悦
a. 変法運動研究の諸課題
b. 湖南変法運動の性格について
c. 楊文会の生涯とその社会観

FUKAZAWA Hideo　深澤秀男
a. 変法運動と中国女学堂
b. 変法運動と湖南瀏陽県致用学堂
c. 中国の近代化と容閎
d. 変法運動と浙江杭州蚕学館

FUKUDA Setsuo　福田節生　　and TSUTSUMI Kazuyoshi　堤和幸
a. 清末山東・江北における水手結社の一動向：幅匪の活動を中心として
b. 清末,長江下流域における巣湖船の活動

FUKUMOTO Masakazu　福本雅一
a. 明末清初　(Kyoto, Dōhōsha, 1984).

FUMA Susumu　夫馬進
a. 善会, 善堂の出発
b. 呂坤の養済院政策
c. 清代松江育嬰堂の経営実態と地方社会
d. 清代前期の育嬰事業

FURUTA Kazuko　古田和子
a. 近代製糸業への社会的対応.

GONJŌ Yasuo　権上康男
a. フランス帝国主義とアジア　(Tokyo, Tokyo University Press, 1985).

GOTŌ Nokuko　後藤延子
a. 民立報期の章士釗

HAGA Noboru　芳賀登
a. 阿片戦争・太平天国・日本

HAGIO Chōichirō　萩尾長一郎
a. 中国旧白話小説戯曲語彙

HAMAGUCHI Masako　浜口允子
a. 清末直隷における諮議局と県議会

HAMASHIMA Atsutoshi 濱島敦俊
a. 中国村廟雑考
b. 北京図書館蔵「葡陽讞牘」簡紹：租佃関係を中心に
c. 明末東南沿海諸省の牢獄
d. 明清時代，中国の地方監獄：初歩的考察
e. 「主佃之分」小考
f. 明清時代の地主佃戸関係と法制
g. 明代中期の「江南商人」について

HAMASHITA Takeshi 浜下武志
a. 近代アジア市場とイギリス
b. 世界資本主義とアジア民族資本
c. 中国幣制改革と外国銀行
d. 近代中国における貿易金融の一考察
e. 資本主義＝植民地体制の形成とアジア
f. 近代アジア貿易圏における銀流通
g. 朝貢貿易システムと近代アジア
h. 東洋文化研究所所蔵中国土地文書目録・解説
(Tokyo, Tōyōgaku bunken sentā sōkan 48, Tokyo University, 1986).

HARADA Masato 原田正己
a. 康有為と日本・東南アジア
b. 康有為の思想運動と民衆 (Tokyo, Tōsui shobō, 1983).

HARASHIMA Haruo 原島春雄
a. 章太炎における学術と革命：「哀」から「寂莫」まで
b. 林則徐小攷

HARIGAYA Miwako 針ヶ谷美和子
a. 太平天国革命期，江浙太湖地域の槍船集団
b. 太平天国占領地域の槍船集団：太湖周辺地域
   を中心にして
c. 太平天国鎮圧後の槍船集団

HARUYAMA Meitetsu 春山明哲
a. 台湾慣習調査と立法問題
b. 植民地における「旧慣」と「法」

HATA Ikuhito 秦惟人
a. 中国の資本主義発生についての最近の中国の研究
b. 近代中国の茶貿易

HATANO Yoshihiro 波多野善大
a. 辛亥革命期の汪兆銘

HAYASHI Kazuo 林和生
a. 中国近世における地方都市の発達：太湖平原烏青鎮
   の場合

HAYASHI Masako 林正子
a. 西仔反と全台団練章程：清末台湾資料の
再検討

HAZAMA Naoki 狭間直樹
a. 孫文思想における民主と独裁

HOKKAIDŌ University, East Asian History Department
a. 抗租闘争の諸問題

HORI Tadashi 堀直
a. 回疆の水資源に関する覚書：「新疆図志」溝渠志の整理を通じて

HORIGUCHI Isamu 堀口修
a.「日清通商航海条約」締結交渉について

HOSHI Ayao 星斌夫
a. 清代初期における賑済諸倉の展開：預備倉と常平倉
b. 中国社会経済史語彙　(Tokyo, Tōyō bunko, 1966).
c. 中国社会福祉政策史の研究 (Tokyo, Kokusho kankōkai, 1985).

HOSOKAWA Kazutoshi 細川一敏
a. "中人"より観た中国郷村の土地所有意議と人間
関係

HOSOYA Yoshio 細合良夫
a. 三藩の乱の再検討：尚可喜一方矢の動何を中心に
b. 雍正朝の正一教
c. 順治康熙朝の正一教

HU Sheng 胡縄, et al.
a. 辛亥革命　(Tokyo, Waseda University Press, 1986).

HUANG Zunsan 黄尊三　(trans. SANETŌ Keishū さねとう けいしゅう
and SATŌ Saburō 三藤三郎)
a. 清国人日本留学日記　(Tokyo, Tōhō shoten, 1986).

HUANG Zongzhi 黄宗智
a. 華北小農経済与社会変遷 (Beijing, Zhonghua shuju).

ICHIKO Chūzō 市古宙三
a. 辛亥革命に関する中国の新刊書

IDO Kazutada 井戸一公
a. 元代の侍衛親軍について：軍の構成・軍官を中心に

IEMURO Shigeo 家室茂雄
a. 清代社倉制度研究序説

IHARA Takushū 伊原沢周
a. 日中両国におけるヘンリージョージの思想の受容：主として孫文・
宮崎民蔵・安部磯雄らの土地論をめぐって

IKEZAWA Miyoshi 池沢実芳
a. 蔣智由の諷刺：「奴才好」から政聞まで

IKUTA Shigeru 生田滋
a. 対外関係からみた琉球古代史：南島稲作史
の理解のために
b. 琉球国の「三山統一」

IMAHORI Seiji 今堀誠二
a. 中国へのアプローチー：その歴史的展開 (Tokyo, Keisō shobō, 1983).

IMAMINATO Yoshinobu 今湊良信
a. 明代中期の「土賊」について

INADA Seiichi 稲田清一
a.「西米東運」考
b. 太平天国前後の客民について

INOUE Susumu 井上進
a. 復社の学

INOUE Tōru 井上徹
a. 黄佐「泰泉郷礼」の世界
b.「郷約」の理念について

ISHIBASHI Hideo 石橋秀雄

a. 征服王朝 清をめぐって

b. 大元 大明 大清時代と五族の中国

c. 清朝小考：八旗雑考.

d. 清初のアハ：太宗天職期を中心に

ISHIBASHI Takao 石橋崇雄

a. 八 gūsaと八 gūsa 色別との成立時期について

b.「宮中檔康熙朝奏摺」（満文諭摺）収録の覚羅
満保奏摺：台湾記事を中心として

ISHIDA Hiroshi 石田浩

a. 中国農村社会経済構造の変容分析

ISHIDA Kenji 石田憲司

a. 明代太和山の経済的基盤について

ISHII Kanji 石井寛治

a. 東アジアにおける帝国主義・講座日本歴史8近代2
(Tokyo, Tokyo University Press, 1985).

ISHII Mayako 石井摩耶子

a. 一八六〇年代の中国におけるイギリス資本の活動：
ジャーディン・マセソン商会の製糸工場経営

ISHII Yōko　石井洋子
a. 辛亥革命期の留日女子学生

ITŌ Kimio　伊藤公夫
a. 中国歴史学界における嘉靖倭寇史研究の動向と
問題点

ITŌ Teruo　伊東昭雄
a. 清仏戦争と東アジア・試論

IWAI Shigeki　岩井茂樹
a. 清代国家財政における中央と地方：酌撥制度を中心として

IWAKABE Yoshimitsu　岩壁義光
a. 日清戦争と居留清国人問題：明治二七年「勅令第百
三十七号」と横浜居留地

IWAMA Kazuo　岩間一雄
a. 明代の思想と社会

IWAMI Hiroshi　岩見宏
a. 明代徭役制度の研究 (Kyoto, Dōhōsha, 1986).

KADA Hirokazu 加宏一
a. 輪船招商局と南京臨時政府

KAGAMI Mitsuyuki 加々美光行
a. 文化大革命と新疆辺境 , in 現代中国のゆく之:
文化大革命の省察　(Tokyo, Ajia keizai kenkyūjo, 1986).

KAMACHI Noriko 蒲地典子
a. 檔案資料にもとづく清代手続法の研究

KANBE Teruo 神戸光軍夫
a. 少数民族の理解をめぐって
b. 雍正朝期の改土帰流について
c. マーガリ事件をめくる英清交渉

KANI Hiroaki 可児弘明
a. 咸豊九(一八五九)年,上海における外国人襲撃事件について
b. 清末の「豬花」から見た中国の鎖国
c. 良賤制度下の蜑戸について

KANO Naoki 狩野直喜
a. 清朝の制度と文学 (Tokyo, Misuzu shobō, 1984).

KASAHARA Tokushi 笠原十九司
a. 日中軍事協定対運動:五四運動前夜における中国

民族運動の展開
b. 日中軍事協定と北京政府の「外蒙自治取消」：ロシア
革命がもたらした東アジア世界の変動の一側面

KATAKURA Yoshikazu 片倉芳和
a. 季雨霖事件について

KATAOKA Kazutada 片山一忠
a. 辛亥革命期の五族共和論をめぐって
b. 清代後期陝西省の差傜について

KATAYAMA Hyōe 片山兵衛
a. 清末内蒙古王府の教育について

KATAYAMA Tomō 片山共夫
a. 元代の士人について

KATAYAMA Tsuyoshi 片山剛
a. 清末広東省珠江デルタの図甲表とそれをめぐる諸問題
b. 清代広東省珠江デルタの図甲制について
c. 清末広東省珠江デルタにおける図甲制の諸矛盾とその改
革（南海県）
d. 清末広東省珠江デルタにおける図甲制の諸矛盾とその
改革（順徳県・香山県）：税糧・戸籍・同族

KATŌ Naoko 加藤直子
a. 民国初期の制銭問題：第一次大戦後の山東を
中心として

KATŌ Yūzō 加藤祐三
a. 黒船前後の世界 (一)：ペリー艦隊の来航
b. ペリー派遣の背景
c. ペリー周辺の人びと
d. 東アジアにおける英米の存在
e. 黒船前後の世界　(Tokyo, Iwanami shoten, 1985).

KAWABATA Genji 河鰭源治
a. 近年の中国における太平天国史の研究

KAWACHI Yoshihiro 河内良弘
a. 明遼陽の東寧衛について

KAWAGOE Yasuhiro 川越泰博
a. 明代衛所官の来衛形態について：玉林衛の場合
b. 明代軍屯制の一考察
c. 明代衛所の舎人について

KAWAKATSU Heita 川勝平太
a. アジア木棉市場の構造と展開

KAWAKATSU Mamoru 川勝守
a. 明・清胥吏政治と民衆
b. 明末,長江デルタ社会と荒政
c. 一九世紀初頭における江南地主経営の一素材：九州大学所蔵「嘉慶租簿」の分析を通して
d. 清代江南の麦租慣行について
e. 一九世紀,蔡経畬堂所有地の小作関係

KAWAKUBO Teirō 川久保悌郎
a. 清代参政考

KAWATA Teiichi 河田悌一
a. 乾嘉の士大夫と考證学：袁枚,孫星衍,戴震そして章学誠

KIM Jong-bak 金鍾博 (trans. Yamane Yukio 山根幸夫 and Inada Hideko 稲田英子)
a. 明代東林党争とその社会背景

KISHI Kazuyuki 岸和行
a. 広東地方社会における無頼像：明末期の珠池盗をめぐって
b. 明代の広東における珠池と珠池盗

KISHIMOTO Mio 岸本美緒
a.「租覈」の土地所有論
b.「歴年記」に見る清初地方社会の生活

KITADA Hidebito 北田英人
a. 中国太湖周辺の「塢」と定住

KOBAYASHI Kazumi 小林一美
a. 斉王氏の反乱：嘉慶白蓮教反乱研究序説
b. 清代の宗教反乱
c. 義和団戦争と明治国家 (Tokyo, Kyūko shoin, 1986).

KOBAYASHI Tomoaki 小林共明
a. 初期の中国対日留学生派遣について：戊戌政変期を中心として
b. 振武学校と留日清国陸軍学生

KOBAYASHI Yoshifumi 小林善文
a. 北京大学と軍閥：蔡元培の改革とそれをめぐる闘争

KOBAYASHI Takeshi 小林武
a. 章炳麟について
b. 清末の任侠

KOGUCHI Hikota 小口彦太
a. 清代中国の刑事裁判における成案の法源性

KOJIMA Shinji 小島晋治
a. 中国から見た明治期の日本

KOJIMA Yoshio 小島淑男
a. 中国国民会について
b. 辛亥革命期蘇州府呉江県の農村手工業
c. 辛亥革命期中国留日学生の動向
d. 辛亥革命と千葉医専

KOKAZE Hidemasa 小風秀雅
a. 帝国主義形成期における日本海運業：日露戦後における東アジア交通網の成立

KONDŌ Kuniyasu 近藤邦康
a. 中国の解放世代と思想史研究：湯志鈞・李沢厚両氏を中心に
b. 中国のユートピア—「大同」, in 夢とビジョン (ed. 木村尚三 , Tokyo, Tokyo University Press, 1985).

KŌSAKA Masanori 香坂昌紀
a. 清代滸野関の研究：滸野関と物貨流通
b. 清代における大運河の物貨流通
c. 清代の餽送

KOTŌ Tomoko 古藤友子
a. 張之洞の中体西用論：「西学」を学ぶ知識人の「倫理」について

KUBOTA Bunji　久保田文次
a. 近代中国像は歪んでいるか
b. 孫文の対日観
c. ふたたび「近代中国像をめぐって
d. 辛亥革命は絶対主義変革か

KUBOTA Hiroko　久保田博子
a. 宋慶齢関係略年譜稿

KURAHASHI Masanao　倉橋正直
a. 営口東盛和事件の裁：清末における商事裁判の一
   事例

KURIHARA Jun　栗原純
a. 清代中部台湾の一考察
b. 清代台湾における米穀移出と郊商人

KURODA Akinobu　黒田明伸
a. 近代中国における権力的改革の再検討
b. 権力的改革の構造とその背景
c. 二十世紀初期揚子江中下流域の貨幣流通

KUROKI Kuniyasu 黒木国泰
a. 一六世紀中国における雇役制確立の歴史的意義

KUSAKA Tsuneo 日下恒夫 and KURAHASHI Yoshihiko 倉橋幸彦
a. 日本における老舎関係文献目録 (Kyoto, Hōyū shoten, 1984).

KUSANO Yasushi 草野靖
a. 中国の地主経済 (Tokyo, Kyūko shoin, 1985).

KUSUNOKI Kendō 楠木監道
a. 明朝の遼東支配と三萬衛：明初の女直軍官をめぐって

KUSUNOSE Masaaki 楠瀬正明
a. 民国初期における知識人の苦悩：黄遠庸を中心として
b. 清末の地方自治論

KUZUDANI Noboru 葛谷登
a. 明末の南京教難における天主教士人の護教の論理

KYŪSHŪ University, East Asian History Department
a. 一九八三年・中国史シンポジウム元明清期における国家"支配"と民衆像の再検討："支配"の中国的特質
(Fukuoka, Kyūshū University Press, 1984).

LI Tingjiang 李廷江
a. 辛亥革命と日本の対応.

LIANG Xizhe 梁希哲 (trans. WADA Masahiro 和田正広)
a. 清世宗の吏治思想についての試論

LIN Lianxiang 林連祥 (trans. FURUDA Shimahiro 古田島洋)
a. 清代小説における科学症候群

LINDLEY, A. F. (trans. KOJIMA Shinji 小島晋治)
a. あるがままの太平軍: その一員として

LIU Jinqing 劉進慶
a. 台湾伝統社会における土地所有の特質に関する一考察

LIU Mingxiu 劉明修
a. 台湾統治と阿片問題 (Tokyo, Yamakawa shuppansha, 1983).

LOU Yulie 楼宇烈
a. 中国近代仏学の振興者

MAEDA Shōtarō 前田勝太郎
a. 広東の辛亥革命

MAEHIRA Fusaaki 真栄平房昭
a. 明清動乱期における琉球貿易の一考察: 康熙慶賀
船の派遣を中心に

MAEYAMA Kanako　前山加奈子
a. 楊昌済と湖南の婦人解放:「結婚論」の番羽訳と
「家族制度改良ノート」について

MANN, Susan (trans. KISHIMOTO Mio　岸本美緒)
a. 清代の社会における寡婦の位置

MASUI Tsuneo　増井経夫
a. 中国の銀と商人 (Tokyo, Kenbun shuppan, 1986).

MATAKICHI Morikiyo　又吉盛清
a. 台湾植民地支配と沖縄(人)

MATSUDA Yoshirō　松田吉郎
a. 広東広州府の米価動向と米穀需給調整:明末より
清中期を中心に
b. 清代台湾中北部の水利事業と一田両主制の成立過程

MATSUMOTO Takaharu　松本隆晴
a. 明代中都建設始末

MATSUMOTO Takehiko　松本武彦
a. 辛亥革命と神戸華僑:武昌蜂起直後における

b. 中華民国華僑統一連合会の成立と性格
c. 辛亥革命時期の在日華僑敢死隊について
d. 対日ボイコットと在日華僑

MATSUNAGA Masayoshi 松永正義
a. 台湾現代小説選 (Tokyo, Kenbun shuppan, 1984).

MATSUURA Akira 松浦章
a. 清代江南船商と沿海航運
b. 清に通報された「島原の乱」の動静

MATSUURA Shigeru 松浦茂
a. 天命年間の世職制度について

MEGURO Katsuhiko 目黒克彦
a. 団練と郷勇との関係について：湘郷団練と湘勇の場合
b. 一九世紀湖南の情勢と変法派の対応
c. 湖南変法運動における保衛局の歴史的位置

MIKI Satoshi 三木聰
a. 清代の福建における抗租の展開
b. 土地革命と「郷族」

MITSUISHI Zenkichi 三石善吉
a. 義和団と「以民制夷」の系譜

b. 派閥と政党

MITSUSHIMA Toku 光島督
a. 清末の川辺経略と川軍の入蔵
b. 清末民初のチベット動乱について

MIURA Hideichi 三浦秀一
a. 湯斌と隆隴其：清初士大夫の人間理解と経世意識
b. 若き日の顔元
c. 顔元の思想

MIYAJIMA Hiroshi 宮嶋博史
a. 方法としての東アジア：東アジア三国における近代への
移行をめぐって

MIYATA Michiaki 宮田道昭
a. 一九世紀半期，中国沿岸部の市場構造

MIYATA Toshihiko 宮田俊彦
a. 琉球・清国交易史 (Tokyo, Daiichi shobō, 1984).

MIZOGUCHI Yūzō 溝口雄三
a. 明清期の人性論
b. 近代中国像は歪んでいないか：洋務と民権および中体西用と
儒教

c. 光緒初期の議会論

MORI Masao 森正夫
a. 明中葉 江南における税糧徴収制度の改革
b. 抗租と奴変 (1981).
c. 「郷族」をめぐって
d. 明初の籍没田について
e. 明初江南における籍没田の形成

MORI Noriko 森紀子
a. 塩場の泰州学派

MORI Tokihiko 森時彦
a. 中国近代化と留学生

MORIOKA Yasu 森岡康
a. 第二次清軍入寇後の朝鮮人捕虜の売買

MORITA Akira 森田明
a. 明末の劉光復と「経野規略」について
b. 明末浙東水利の一考察：諸曁地方を中心として
c. 清代常州の浚河事業について

d. 清末民初の江南デルタ水利と帝国主義支配：上海「浚浦局」の成立について
e. 清末上海の河工事業と地方自治
f. 明末清初における福建晋江の施氏

MORITA Shigemitsu 森田成滿
a. 清代土地所有権法研究 (Tokyo, Keisō shobō, 1984).

MOTONO Eiichi 本野英一
a. アロー戦争後の長江中下流域の信用構造と世界市場：アメリカ南北戦争の影響を中心に

MUKŌYAMA Hiroo 向山寛夫
a. 日本治下における台湾の法と政治：民族法学の視点に立って

MURAO Susumu 村尾進
a. カントン学海堂の知識人とアヘン弛禁論 厳禁論

MURAYAMA Naoko 村山直子
a.「聖朝破邪集」に見られる明末の反キリスト教運動について

NAGAI Kazumi 永井算己
a. 中国近代政治史論叢 (Tokyo, Kyūko shoin, 1983).

NAGAI Nobuhiro　長井伸浩
a. 洋務運動期の官督商辨制度：直隷開平礦務局を
例として

NAGANO Shin'ichirō　永野慎一郎
a. アロー号事件をめぐるイギリス議会論争
b. イギリスの太平天国政策

NAGASE Mamoru　長瀬守
a. 政治文化からみた清・琉球関係の展開

NAGOYA University, East Asian History Department
a. 地域社会の視点：地域社会とリーダー

NAKADA Yoshinobu　中田吉信
a. 中国における杜文秀の評価をめぐって
b. 「漢奸」から「愛国者」へ

NAKAGAWA Yasuko　中川靖子
a. 「通商彙纂」中国関係記事目録
b. 清末直隷における新政の事例

NAKAI Hideki　中井英基
a. 清末民国初における股有份限公司の経営体質

NAKAMURA Fujie 中村ふじゑ
a. ピスワリスの墓碑銘：高永清さんを偲んで

NAKAMURA Jihee 中村治兵衛
a. 明代の河泊所と漁民
b. 山西の農村をめぐる二三問題, in 中央大学百周
年記念論文集 (Tokyo, Chūō University, 1985).
c. 明初の魚課と河泊所官の地域廻避

NAKAMURA Satoru 中村耳谷
a. 康有為における経書の認識：経学と西学受容との関係を中心にて

NAKAMURA Tadashi 中村義
a. 第一回在華イギリス商業会所会議
b. 華訳「明治維新史」覚書
c. 成城学校と中国人留学生
d. 嘉納治五郎と楊度
e. 清末幣制論

NAKAMURA Takashi 中村孝志
a. 福州の台湾籍民：一九〇九年における

NAKAMURA Tetsuo 中村哲夫
a. 近代中国社会史研究序説 (Tokyo, Yoshikawa kōbunkan, 1985).

NAKAYAMA Yoshihiro 中山義弘
a. 近代中国における女性解放の思想と行動 (Kita Kyūshū, Kita Kyūshū Chūgoku shoten, 1983).
b. 浙江辛亥革命における政治展開と国家統一

NAMIKI Yorihisa 並木頼寿
a. 清代河南省の漕糧について
b. 一八五〇年代, 河南聯荘会の抗糧暴動
c. 太平天国期の華北

NARAKINO Shimesu 楢木野宣
a. 清代の地方政治における北と南

NATSUI Haruki 夏井春喜
a. 太平天国時期蘇州における土豪的支配について
b. 太平天国後の蘇州における小作料徴収関係について：租冊史料の分析を通して
c. 太平天国後の浙西における客民の問題について
d. 清末蘇州の地主：佃戸関係について

NISHI Junzō 西順蔵 and KOJIMA Shinji 小島晋治
a. アジアの差別問題 (Tokyo, Akashi shoten, 1986).

NISHIMURA Kazuyo 西村かずよ
a. 明末清初の奴僕について

NISHIMURA Kōjirō 西村幸次郎
a. 中国における法の継承性論争 (Tokyo, Waseda hikaku hō
kenkyūjo, 1983).

NISHIMURA Shigeo 西村成雄
a. 中国近代東北地域史研究 (Tokyo, Hōritsu bunka sha,
1984)

NISHIZATO Yoshiyuki 西里喜行
a. 王韜と循環日報について
b. 苦力貿易とロバート・バウン号事件

NOGUCHI Tetsurō 野口鉄郎
a. 紅蓮教と哥老会
b.「斎匪」と「会匪」
c. 明清時代の「邪教」結社と民衆
d. 明代白蓮教史の研究 (Tokyo, Yūzankaku, 1986).

NOGUCHI Yoshitaka 野口善敬
a. 明末の仏教居士黄端伯を巡って

NOMURA Tōru　野村亨
a. 淞滬鉄道に関する一考察

NORIMATSU Akifumi　則松彰文
a. 雍正期における米穀流通と米価変動

NOZAWA Yutaka　野沢豊
a. 五四運動と省議会：民族運動の内部構造の検討
　　にむけて
b. 民国初期，袁世凱政権の経済政策と張謇

OGATA Yasushi　尾形康
a. 王國維あるいは飛躍の諸形式
b. 厳復とミル論理学

OGATA Yasushi　緒形康
a. 清末進化論の思想的位置とその帰趨

OGAWA Tamaki　小川環樹, NISHIDA Taichirō　西田太一郎　, and
　AKATSUKA Kiyoshi　赤塚忠
a. 新字源 (Tokyo, Kadogawa shoten, 1977).

OH Keum-sung (O Gûm-sông) 吳金成　(trans. YAMANE Yukio　山根
　幸夫)
a. 明代紳士層の社会移動について

b. 中国近世社会経済史研究 (Seoul, Iljogak, 1986).

OKAMATSU Santarō 岡松参太郎
a. 台湾私法
b. 台湾慣習記事

ŌKI Yasushi 大木康
a. 明末における白話小説の作者と読者について:石幾部彰紙の所説に寄せて

ŌKUMA Akiko 大隈晶子
a. 明代山東省における條鞭便法について
b. 明代永楽期における朝貢について

OKUYAMA Norio 奥山憲夫
a. 明代巡撫制度の変遷

OKUZAKI Yūji 奥崎裕司
a. 明末清初の利殖規範:功過格の一側面
b. 清末の地主・佃農関係:善書の諸例の検討
c. 清末の善書における民衆の生き方:アヘン戦争から太平天国まで

ONO Kazuko 小野和子
a. 東林党と張居正
b. 東林党考(二):その形成過程をめぐって
c. 山西商人と張居正

ŌNO Miboko　大野美穂子
a. 上海における戯園の形成と発展

ŌNO Santoku　大野三徳
a. 国民革命期に至る栄家企業の展開とその性格

ŌSATO Hiroaki　大里浩秋
a. 陶成章年譜 (稿)

ŌSAWA Akihiro　大澤顯浩
a. 明末宗教的反乱の一考察

ŌTANI Toshio　大谷敏夫
a. 清代郷紳の理念と現実
b. 揚州・常州学術考：その社会的関連
c. 清朝政治構造と士大夫
d. 清朝君主権と士大夫
e. 陶澍・林則徐の江南統治策について
f. 清末湖南官僚形成過程について
g. 洋務運動期における経世思想についての一考察
h. 林則徐研究における現状と課題

OYAMA Masaaki　小山正明
a. 文書史料からみた明・清時代徽州府下の奴婢・
　 庄僕制

OZAWA Junko 小沢純子
a. 一八五二年厦門暴動について

PAK Jong-hyûn 朴鍾玄
a. 十九世紀末中国改革論者の聯盟論について

PAN Liangzhi 潘良熾
a. 明初官吏考核制度述評

REKISHIGAKU kenkyūkai 歴史学研究会
a. 現代アジアへの視点, アジア現代史別巻 (Tokyo, Aoki shoten, 1985).

RINBARA Fumiko 林原文子
a. 愛国布の誕生について

SAEKI Yūichi 佐伯有一
a. 「長隨論」攷: 長隨に関する一史料をめぐって
b. 明清交替期の胥吏像一斑

SAITŌ Michihiko 斉藤道彦
a. 李大釗研究史覚書・中国編

SAKAI Tadao 酒井忠夫
a. 中国史上の垠と流垠

SAKAIDE Yoshinobu 坂出祥伸
a. 清末における科学教育：上海・格致書院の場合
b. 中国近代の思想と科学 (Kyoto, Dōhōsha, 1983).
c. 康有為 (Tokyo, Shūeisha, 1985).

SAKAMOTO Hiroko 坂元ひろ子
a. 中国近代思想の一断面：譚嗣同の以太（エーテル）論
b. 章炳麟の個の思想と唯識仏教

SAKUMA Shigeo 佐久間重男
a. 景徳鎮の督陶官唐英について
b. 清代前期の景徳鎮窯業

SANADA Takehiko 真田武彦
a. 明代正徳期における藍廷瑞の乱について

SASAKI Hiroshi 佐々木寛
a. 練軍について

SASAKI Mamoru 佐々木衛
a. 山東義和団運動の社会的性格

SASAKI Masaya 佐々木正哉
a. 鴉片戦争の研究：ポティンデャーの着任から南京条約の締結まで"

b. 酉陽教案補遺
c. 中国における共和思想の展開と台湾民主国独立運動始末
d. 一八七一年広東・福建・湖広地方の仇教謡言掲帖

SASAKI Tatsuo 佐々木達夫
a. 元明時代窯業史研究　(Tokyo, Yoshikawa kōbunkan, 1985).

SASAKI Yō 佐々木揚
a. 同治年間における清朝官人の対日観について：日清修好
　条規締結に至る時期を中心として
b. 同治年間における清朝洋務派の日本論
c. 日清戦争期より

SATŌ Akiko 佐藤明子
a. 上海製糸女工に関する一考察：一九二〇年代前半における

SATŌ Fumitoshi 佐藤文俊
a. 明末農民反乱と掌盤子
b. 明末農民反乱の研究　(Tokyo, Kenbun shuppan, 1985).

SATŌ Kimihiko 佐藤公彦
a. 清代白蓮教の史的展開：八卦教と諸反乱
b. 一八九一年熱河の金丹道蜂起

SATŌ Manabu　佐藤学
a. 明初北京への富民層強制移住について
b. 明代北京における鋪戸の役とその銀納化：都市商工業
者の実態と把握をめぐって
c. 明代南京における鋪戸の役とその改革

SATŌ Saburō　佐藤三郎
a. 近代日中交渉史の研究　(Tokyo, Yoshikawa kōbunkan, 1984).

SATŌ Shin'ichi　佐藤慎一
a. 一八九〇年代の「民権」論：張之洞と何啓の「論争」を中心に
b. 鄭観応について(二)：「万国公法」と「商戦」

SATŌ Yutaka　佐藤豊
a. 章炳麟 進化論ノート

SAWAYA Harutsugu　沢谷昭次
a. 「中国史研究入門」の現状

SEGAWA Masahisa　瀬川昌久
a. 客家と本地

SEINEN Chūgoku kenkyūsha kaigi　青年中国研究者会議
a. 続中国民衆反乱の世界　(Tokyo, Kyūko shoin, 1983).

SHIBA Yoshinobu 斯波義信
a.「麻渓改壩烏橋始末記」について
b.「湘湖水利志」と「湘湖考略」：浙江蕭山県湘湖の水利始末
c. 中国における資本主義の展開と都市化

SHIBAHARA Takuji 芝原拓自
a. 東アジアにおける近代，講座日本歴史7近代1 (Tokyo, Tokyo University Press).
b. 日中両国の綿製品・生糸貿易とその背景

SHIGA Shūzō 滋賀秀三
a. 清代中国の法と裁判 (Tokyo, Sōbunsha, 1984).
b. 崇明島の承価と過投

SHIMA Ichirō 島一郎
a. 近代中国における民族機械工業の展開：その沿革と生産構造

SHIMADA Kenji 島田虔次
a. アジア歴史研究入門 (Kyoto, Dōhōsha, 1983).

SHIMADA Masarō 島田正郎
a. 明・韃靼鞄門の規矩条約

SHIMAMOTO Nobuko 嶋本信子
a. 白朗の乱

SHINMURA Ireko 新村容子
a. 清末四川省における局士の歴史的性格

SHINOZAKI Moritoshi 篠崎守利
a. "湖南変法"時代の楊篤生

SHIROI Takashi 城井隆志
a. 万暦期の政治党派と士大夫：万暦二十年代の吏部について
b. 万暦三十年代における沈一貫の政治と党争
c. 嘉靖初年の翰林院改革について

SŌDA Hiroshi 相田洋
a. 羅教の成立とその展開
b. 明代における体制イデオロギーと民衆思想

SŌDA Saburō 曽田三郎
a. 生糸の世界市場における上海器械糸
b. 辛亥革命前の諸改革と湖南

SON Bun kenkyūkai 孫文研究会
a. 孫中山研究 日中国際学術討論会報告集 (Tokyo,

Hōritsu bunkasha, 1986).

SUETSUGU Reiko 末次玲子
a. 五四時期の婦人運動素描
b. 五四時期の中国婦人運動とロシア革命認識

SUGIHARA Kaoru 杉原薫
a. アジア間貿易の形成と構造

SUGIYAMA Nobuya 杉山伸也
a. 東アジアにおける「外圧」の構造

SUZUI Masataka 鈴井正孝
a. 清初の編審制度と起丁方法について

SUZUKI Ken'ichi 鈴木健一
a. 旅順工科学堂について

SUZUKI Tomoo 鈴木智夫
a. 不平等条約と洋務派
b. 草創期広東製糸業の経営特質:「循環日報」の「告白」より見る
c. 洋務運動期における近代綿業移植論の研究
d. 中国における近代工業の形成と洋務派
e. 近代産業の移植と李鴻章

f. 明清時代江浙農民の杭州進香について

g. 洋務運動期における上海生糸貿易の展開

TAGA Akigorō 多賀秋五郎

a. 中国における新学制実施前夜の族塾について

TAJIRI Toshi 田尻利

a. 戦前期のわが国における洋務運動の評価について,

in 創立五十周年記念論文集 (Kagoshima keidai, 1984).

TAKADA Atsushi 高田淳

a. 清末における王船山

b. 辛亥革命と章炳麟の斉物哲学 (Tokyo, Kenbun
shuppan, 1984).

TAKAHASHI Akira 高橋章

a. ジョン・ヘイの第二次門戸解放通牒.

TAKAHASHI Kōsuke 高橋孝助

a. 近代初期の上海における善堂: その「都市」的状況の
対応の側面について

b. 善堂研究に関する一視点:上海の善堂を手がかりとして

c. "商賈の道"を以企業を興す:夏東元「鄭観応伝」を読む

d. 滬北棲流公所の成立

TAKINO Shōjirō 滝野正二郎
a. 清代 淮安関 の 構成 と 機能 について

TANAKA Issei 田仲一成
a. 中国 の 宗族 と 演劇 (Tokyo, Tokyo University Press, 1985).
b. 明末文人 の 戯曲観
c. 清代浙東宗族 の 組織 形成 における 宗祠 演劇 について

TANAKA Masatoshi 田中正俊
a. 明・清時代 の 問屋制 前貸生産 について：衣料生産 を
   主 とする研究史的 覚え書
b. 文学 の 思想性 と 歴史 を 視る 眼 と：アジア史 の 認識 に 向けて

TANG Zhijun 湯志鈞
a. 辛亥革命 と 章炳麟 (trans. KONDŌ Kuniyasu 近藤邦康)
b. 近代中国 の 革命思想 と 日本 (trans. KONO Michiko 兒野
   道子, Tokyo, Nihon keizai hyōronsha, 1986).

TANG Zhijun and KONDŌ Kuniyasu 近藤邦康
a. 中国近代 の 思想家 (Tokyo, Iwanami shoten, 1985).

TANI Mitsutaka 谷光隆
a. 黄 淮交匯 と 楊一魁 の 河工

TANIGUCHI Fusao 谷口房男
a. 嘉靖海寇反乱掃討 と 瓦氏夫人

TANIGUCHI Kikuo 谷口規矩雄
a. 呂坤の土地丈量策と郷村改革について
b. 呂坤の郷甲法について
c. 地丁併徴の一側面
d. 東陽民変

TERADA Hiroaki 寺田浩明
a. 田面田底慣行の法的性格：概念的な分析を中心として
b. 「崇明県志」に見える「承価」「過投」「頂首」について

TERADA Takanobu 寺田隆信
a. 明代泉州回族雑考
b. 山西票号覚書

TERAHIRO Teruo 寺広映雄
a. 孫文のヨーロッパにおける革命活動

TESSAN Hiroshi 鉄山博
a. 清末四川における半植民地化と仇教運動
b. 一八九一年熱河朝陽起義の一考察
c. 「成都教案」小考

TOKUNAGA Masajirō 徳永正二郎
a. 為替と信用：国際決済制度の史的展開 (Tokyo, Shin hyōron, 1976).

TOMITA Noboru 富田昇
a. 譚嗣同の人間観：網羅衝決論を中心に
b. 李大釗、日本留学時代の思想形成：「民彝」概念の成立をめぐって

TŌYŌ shi kenkyūkai 東洋史研究会
a. 雍正時代の研究 (Kyoto, Dōhōsha, 1986).

TSUKADA Shigeyuki 塚田誠之
a. 明清時代における壮 (Zhuang) 族の佃農化に関する一考察

TSUKASE Susumu 塚瀬進
a. 辛亥革命期における漢冶萍公司日中合弁問題について

TSUNOYAMA Sakae 角山栄
a. 日本領事報告の研究 (Tokyo, Dōbunkan, 1986).

TSUNOYAMA Sakae and TAKASHIMA Masaaki 高嶋雅明
a. マイクロフィルム版領事報告資料収録目録 (Tokyo, Yūshōdō shuppan, 1985).

TSURUMI Naohiro 鶴見尚弘
a. 魚鱗冊を訪ねて：中国研修の旅

UCHIYAMA Masao 内山雅生
a. 日本を見ることと中国を見ること

b. 民国初期, 華北農村における験契の実施と民衆運動

UEDA Makoto 上田信
a. 地域の履歴
b. 地域と宗族：浙江省山間部
c. 村に作用する磁力について

USUI Katsumi 臼井勝美
a. 中国をめぐる近代日本外交 (Tokyo, Chikuma shobō, 1983).

USUI Sachiko 臼井佐知子
a. 太平天国末期における李鴻章の軍事費対策
b. 同治四 (一八六五) 年, 江蘇省における賦税改革

USUI Takashi 臼井丘
a. 清朝中期における収元教の系譜

USUI Yasuko 臼井健子
a. 頼文光：太平天国から捻軍へ

WADA Hironori 和田博徳
a. 里甲制と里社壇・郷厲壇

WADA Masahiro 和田正広
a. 明代科挙制度と士大夫

b. 明代 科挙 官僚家系の連続的側面に関する一考察
c. 李成梁 権力における財政的基盤
d. 明代の地方官ポストにおける身分制序列に関する一考察
e. 李成梁一族の軍事的台頭

WAKABAYASHI Masafumi 若林正丈
a. 総督政治と台湾土着地主資産階級：公立台中
中学校設立問題，一九一二～一九一五年
b. 台湾抗日運動史研究 (Tokyo, Kenbun shuppan, 1983).

WAKAMORI Tamio 和歌森民男
a. 資料紹介：高永清「回想録」：霧社事件とその研究にふれて

WANG Lianmao 王連茂 (trans. MIKI Satoshi 三木聰)
a. 明末泉州の佃租収奪と「斗梘会」闘争

WANG Qingcheng 王慶成
a.「天父聖旨」,「天兄聖書」と太平天国の歴史

WANG Songxing 王崧興 and SEGAWA Masahisa 瀬川昌久
a. 漢民族の移民とエスニシティー：香港・台湾の事例をもとに

WANG Xiaolian 王孝廉
a. 辱棲志：清代 譴責小説の先駆

WATANABE Atsushi 渡辺惇

a. 清代秘密結社と民衆：長江下流域を中心として
b. 河東塩政改革と白蓮教の乱
c. 近代中国における秘密結社

WATANABE Tadase 渡部忠世 and IKUTA Shigeru 生田滋

a. 南島の稲作文化 (Tokyo, Hōdai shuppankyoku, 1984).

WATANABE Tadase and SAKURAI Yumio 桜井由躬雄

a. 中国江南の稲作文化：その学際的研究 (Tokyo, NHK, 1984).

WATARU Masahiro 渡昌弘

a. 明代洪武年間の制挙
b. 明初捐納入監概観

XU Dingxin 徐鼎新 (trans. KURAHASHI Masanao 倉橋正直)

a. 旧中国の商会のみなもと

YAMADA Kōichirō 山田耕一郎

a. 清初の捐納

YAMADA Masaru 山田賢

a. 清代の移住民社会

YAMAMOTO Eiji 山本英史
a. 清初華北における丁税科派についての一見解

YAMANA Hirofumi 山名弘史
a. 潘曽斤について

YAMANE Yukio 山根幸夫
a. 新編辛亥革命文献目録 (Tokyo, Ryōgen shoten, 1983).
b. 廿一箇条交渉と日本人の対応
c. 中国史研究入門 (Tokyo, Yamakawa shuppansha, 1983).
d. 清代山東の市集と紳士層
e. 袁世凱と日本人たち

YASUDA Tōru 安田淳
a. 中国の第一次大戦参戦問題

YASUNO Shōzō 安野省三
a. 中国の異端・無頼

YOKOYAMA Hiroaki 横山宏章
a. 中国の共和革命運動と秘密結社

YOKOYAMA Suguru 横山英
a. 二〇世紀初期の地方政治近代化について覚書 , in
中国の近代化と地方政治 (Tokyo, Keisō shobō, 1985).

b. 清末ナショナリズムと国家有機体説

YOSHIDA Kin'ichi 吉田金一
a. ロシアの東方進出とネルチンスク条約　(Tokyo, Kindai Chūgoku kenkyū sentā, 1984).

YOSHIDA Kōichi 吉田浤一
a. 日本における中国近現代経済史研究の動向(1)：農業を中心として

YOSHIDA Tora 吉田寅
a. 入華宣教師アーバーの「大徳国学校論略」について
b. プロテスタント宣教師マルティンの西学紹介と中国文著作

YOSHINAMI Kōji 好並隆司
a. 近世・山西の水争をめぐって：晋水・県東両渠の場合

YOSHIO Hiroshi 吉尾寛
a. 明末流賊研究についての覚書
b. 「楊文弱先生集」について：張顕清の所説によせて
c. 明末・楊嗣昌の「剿餉」案について

YOSHIOKA Yoshinobu 吉岡義信
a. 明代寧夏の水利について

ZENG Dexiang 曾德興
a. 清末の切音字運動に関する一考察

Journals Cited

Aichi gakuin daigaku bungakubu kiyō
愛知学院大学文学部紀要

Aichi daigaku kokusai mondai kenkyūjo kiyō
愛知大学 国際 問題 研究所紀要

Aichi kenritsu daigaku bungaku ronshū 愛知県立大学文学論集

Aichi kyōiku daigaku kenkyū hōkoku 愛知教育大学研究報告

Ajia keizai アジア経済

Ajia kenkyū アジア研究

Aoyama shigaku 青山史学

Arutesu riberaresu アルテス リベラレス

Atarashii rekishigaku to tame ni 新しい歴史学のために

Bunka 文化

Byōtōō 猫頭鷹

Chiba daigaku hōgaku ronshū 千葉大学法学論集

Chiba shigaku 千葉史学

Chikaki ni arite 近きに在りて

Chiiki bunka kenkyū 地域文化研究

Chōsen gakuhō 朝鮮学報

Chūgoku kenkyū geppō 中国研究月報

Chūgoku kindai shi kenkyū 中国近代史研究

Chūgoku kindai shi kenkyū tsūshin 中国近代史研究通信

Chūgoku--shakai to bunka 中国一社会と文化

Chūgoku shi kenkyū　中国史研究

Chūtetsu bungaku kaihō　中哲文学会報

Chūō daigaku bungakubu kiyō　中央大学文学部紀要

Chūō daigaku daigakuin ronkyū--bungaku kenkyū kahen
中央大学大学院論究：文学部研究科編

Chūō daigaku jimbun kenkyū kiyō　中央大学人文研究紀要

Chūō gakuin daigaku ronsō　中央学院大学論叢

Chūō shigaku　中央史学

Daidō bunka daigaku Tōyō kenkyū　大同文化大学東洋研究

Daitō bunka daigaku keizai ronshū　大東文化大学経済論集

Eikyoshū　盈虚集

Fukuoka daigaku sōgō kenkyūjohō　福岡大学総合研究所報

Fukuoka joshi tandai kiyō　福岡女子短大紀要

Gakushūin daigaku bungakubu kenkyū nempō
学習院大学文学部研究年報

Gendai Chūgoku　現代中国

Gifu daigaku kyōiku gakubu kenkyū hōkoku--jimbun kagaku
岐阜大学教育学部研究報告：人文科学

Hikaku bungaku kenkyū　比較文学研究

Hirosaki daigaku jimbun gakubu bunkei ronsō
弘前大学人文学部文経論叢

Hiroshima daigaku bungakubu kiyō　広島大学文学部紀要

Hiroshima daigaku Tōyō shi kenkyūshitsu hōkoku
広島大学東洋史研究室報告

Hitotsubashi ronsō　一橋論叢

Hōgaku　法学

Hokkaidō daigaku bungakubu kiyō　北海島大学文学部紀要

Hokkaidō kyōiku daigaku kiyō--shakai kagaku hen
北海島教育大学紀要一社会科学編

Hōritsu ronsō Meiji daigaku hōritsu kenkyūjo
法律論叢明治大学法律研究所

Hōsei shigaku　法政史学

Hōsei shi kenkyū　法政史研究

Jimbun gakka ronshū　人文学科論集

Jimbun kenkyū (Ōsaka shiritsu daigaku bungakubu kiyō)
人文研究 大阪市立大学文学部紀要

Jimbun ronsō　人文論叢

Jūtaku kenchiku　住宅建築

Kadai shigaku　鹿大史学

Kagoshima daigaku hōbungakubu kiyō--jimbun kagaku ronshū
鹿児島大学法文学部 紀要一人文科学論集

Kainan shigaku　海南史学

Kansai daigaku bungaku ronshū　関西大学文学論集

Kansai daigaku keizai ronshū　関西大学経済論集

Kansai daigaku Tōzai gakujutsu kenkyū kiyō
関西大学東西学術研究紀要

Keiō gijuku daigaku daigakuin hōgaku kenkyū ronbunshū
慶応義塾大学大学院法学研究論文集

Keizaigaku ronsō　経済学論叢

Keizai shūshi　経済集志

Kikan sanzenri 季刊三千里

Kikan Tōzai kōshō 季刊東西交歩

Kindai Chūgoku 近代中国

Kindai Chūgoku kenkyū ihō 近代中国研究彙報

Kōbe daigaku shigaku nempō 神戸大学史学年報

Kōchi kōgyō kōtō senmon gakkō gakujutsu kiyō
高知工業高等専門学校学術紀要

Kōgakkan ronsō 皇学館論叢

Kokugakuin hōgaku 国学館法学

Kokusai seiji 国際政事

Kokushikan daigaku bungakubu jimbun gakkai kiyō
国士館大学文学部人文学会紀要

Kokushikan daigaku kyōyō ronshū 国士館大学教養論集

Komazawa daigaku gaikokugo kenkyū ronshū
駒沢大学外国語研究論集

Kōnan joshi tanki daigaku kiyō 江南女子短期大学紀要

Kumamoto daigaku bungakubu ronsō, shigaku
熊本大学文学部論叢, 史学

Kumatsu shū 呴沫集

Kyōikugaku ronshū 教育学論集

Kyōto sangyō daigaku ronshū 京都産業大学論集

Kyūshū shigaku 九州史学

Meiji gakuin daigaku hōgaku kenkyū 明治学院大学法学研究

Mindai shi kenkyū 明代史研究

Minzokugaku kenkyū 民族学研究

Miyajiro kyōiku daigaku kiyo 宮城教育大学紀要

Nagoya daigaku bungakubu kenkyū kiyo ronshū (shigaku)
名古屋大学 文学部研究紀要論集 史学

Nagoya daigaku Tōyō shi kenkyū hōkoku 名古屋大学 東洋史研究報告

Nampō bunka 南方

Nihon Chūgoku gakkai hō 日本中国学会報

Nihon daigaku keizai gakubu keizai kagaku kenkyūjo kiyō
日本大学経済学部経済科学研究所紀要

Ochanomizu shigaku お茶の水史学

Ochanomizu joshi daigaku jimbun kagaku kiyō
お茶の水女子大学人文科学紀要

Oikonomika おいこのみか

Okayama daigaku hōgakkai zasshi 岡山大学法学会雑誌.

Ōsaka kyōiku daigaku shakai kagaku seikatsu kagaku kiyō
大阪教育大学社会科学生活科学紀要

Rekishi 歴史

Rekishigaku kenkyū 歴史学研究

Rekishi hyōron 歴史評論

Rekishi kagaku to kyōiku 歴史科学と教育

Rekishi kōron 歴史公論

Rekishi to shakai 歴史と社会

Rinrigaku 倫理学

Ritsumeikan hōgaku 立命館法学

Rōhyakusei no sekai 老百姓の世界

Ryūkyū daigaku kyōiku gakubu kiyō 琉球大学教育学部紀要

Saga daigaku kyōiku gakubu kenkyū ronbunshū
佐賀大学 教育学部 研究 論文集

Sakai joshi tanki daigaku kiyō 堺女子短期大学紀要

Seiji keizai shigaku 政治経済史学

Seinan gakuin daigaku bunri ronshū 西南学院大学文理論集

Sekai shi no kenkyū 世界史の研究

Shakai kagaku tōkyū 社会科学討究

Shakai keizai shigaku 社会経済史学

Shichō 史潮

Shidoku 史読

Shien 史淵

Shigaku 史学

Shigaku kenkyū 史学研究

Shigaku kenshū 史学研修

Shigaku zasshi 史学雑誌.

Shihō 史朋

Shikai 史海

Shikyō 史境

Shingai kakumei kenkyū 辛亥革命研究

Shin Okinawa bungaku 新沖縄文学

Shinshū daigaku jimbun gakubu jimbun kagaku ronshū
信州大学人文学部人文科学論集

Shirin 史林

Shiron 史論

Shisō 思想

Shisō* 史窓

Shiyū 史友

Shūjitsu joshi daigaku shigaku ronshū
就実女子大学史学論集

Shūkan Tōyōgaku 集刊東洋学

Shundai shigaku 駿台史学

Taiwan kin-gendai shi kenkyū 台湾近現代史研究

Tetsugaku nempō 哲学年報

Tetsugaku shisō ronshū 哲学思想論集

Tō-A 東亜

Tochi seido shigaku 土地制度史学

Tōhōgaku 東方学

Tōhō gakuhō 東方学報

Tōhō gakuen daigaku tanki daigakubu kiyō
桐朋学園大学短期大学部紀要

Tōhoku daigaku Tōyō shi ronshū 東北大学東洋史論集

Tōhoku gakuin daigaku ronshū 東北学院大学論集

Tōkai daigaku bungakubu kiyō 東海大学文学部紀要

Tōkyō keidai gakkai shi 東京経大学会誌

Toyama daigaku jimbun gakubu kiyō 富山大学人文学部紀要

Tōyō bunka 東洋文化

Tōyō bunka kenkyūjo kiyō 東洋文化研究所紀要

Tōyō daigaku daigakuin kiyō 東洋大学大学院紀要

Tōyō daigaku bungakubu kiyō 東洋大学文学部紀要

Tōyō daigaku Tōyō shi kenkyū hōkoku
東洋大学東洋史研究報造

Tōyō gakuhō 東洋学報

Tōyō gakujutsu kenkyū 東洋学術研究

Tōyō shi kenkyū 東洋史研究

Tōyō shi ronshū 東洋史論集

Tōyō tōji 東洋陶磁

Waseda daigaku daigakuin bungaku kenkyūka kiyō
早稲田大学大学院文学研究科紀要

Yahata daigaku ronshū 八幡大学論集

Yahata daigaku shakai bunka kenkyūjo kiyō
八幡大学社会文化研究所紀要

Yamagata daigaku shigaku ronshū 山形大学史学論集

Yokohama shiritsu daigaku ronsō--jimbun kagaku keiretsu
横浜市立大学論叢一人文科学系列

Collections of Essays Cited

Chūgoku bunka:

Chūgoku shijō yori mita Chūgoku bunka no dempa to bunka henyō

中国史上より見た中国文化の伝播と文化変容 (The
Diffusion of Chinese Culture in Chinese History and Cultural
Transformation), Tokyo, 1984.

Chūgoku kinsei:

Chūgoku kinsei no toshi to bunka 中国近世の都市と文化
(City and Culture in Early Modern China), ed. Umehara Kaoru
梅原郁 Kyoto, Kyōto daigaku jimbun kagaku kenkyūjo, 1984.

Chūgoku shitaifu:

Chūgoku shitaifu kaikyū to chiiku shakai to no kankei ni tsuite no
sōgō teki kenkyū 中国士大夫階級と地域社会との関係
について総合的研究 (Cumulative Research on the
Relationship Between the Literati Class and Local Society in
China), ed. Tanigawa Michio 谷川道雄, Kyoto, Kyoto
University, 1983.

Chūsei:

Chūsei no minshū undō 中世の民衆運動 (Medieval Popular
Movements), vol. 7 of Chūsei shi kōzā 中世史講座 (Essays
on Medieval History), ed. Kimura Shōzaburō 木村尚三郎
Tokyo, Gakuseisha, 1985.

Masubuchi:

Chūgoku shi ni okeru shakai to minshū: Masubuchi Tatsuo sensei
taikan kinen ronshū 中国史における社会と民衆：増淵龍
夫先生退官記念論集 (Society and the People in Chinese
History: Essays Commemorating the Retirement of Professor
Masubuchi Tatsuo), Tokyo, Kyūko shoin, 1983.

Henkakki:

Henkakki Ajia no hō to keizai 変革期アジアの法と経済 (Asian
Law and Economy in Transformation), ed. Kikuchi Hideo 菊地
英夫 , Tokyo, "Report on Research Findings Subsidized by
Scientific Research Funds for the Years 1983-85."

Higashi:

Higashi Ajia sekai shi tankyū 東アジア世界史探究
(Examination of the World of East Asia), ed. Teng Weicao 滕
維藻, Wang Zhongluo 王仲犖 , Okuzaki Yūji 奥崎裕司
and Kobayashi Kazumi 小林一美 , Tokyo, Kyūko shoin, 1986.

Kenryoku:

Jūseiki ikō nijisseiki shotō ni itaru Chūgoku shakai no kenryoku
kōzō ni kansuru sōgō teki kenkyū 十世紀以降 二十世紀
初頭に至る中国社会の権力構造に関する総合的研究
(Joint Research on the Structure of Power in Chinese Society
from the 10th through the Early 20th Centuries), Kyoto, Kyoto
University, 1985.

Kikuchi:

Kikuchi Takaharu sensei tsuitō ronshū: Chūgoku kin-gendai ronshū
菊地貴晴先生追悼論集：中国近現代論集 (Essays in
Memory of Professor Kikuchi Takaharu on Modern and Contemporary
China), Tokyo, Kyūko shoin, 1985.

Migami:

Migami Tsugio hakase kiju kinen ronbunshū rekishi tōji kōko
三上次男博士喜寿記念論文集歴史陶磁考古 (Essays
on History, Pottery, and Archeology Commemorating Professor
Migami Tsugio's 77th Birthday), Tokyo, Heibonsha, 1985.

Min-Shin jidai:

Min-Shin jidai no seiji to shakai 明清時代の政治と社会
(Politics and Society in the Ming-Qing Period), ed. Ono Kazuko,
Kyoto, Jimbun kakagu kenkyūjo, Kyoto University, 1983.

Nakamura:

Nakamura Jihee sensei koki kinen Tōyō shi ronsō 中村治兵衛
先生古稀記念東洋史論叢 (Essays in East Asian
History Commemorating the 70th Birthday of Professor Nakamura
Jihee), Tokyo, Tōsei shobō, 1986.

Ningensei:

Chūgoku ni okeru ningensei no tankyū 中国における人間性の
探求 (In Pursuit of Human Nature in China), ed. Kanaya Osamu
金谷治, Tokyo, Sōbunsha, 1983.

Nishi:

Nishi to higashi to: Maejima Shinji sensei tsuitō ronbunshū 西と
東と:前島信次先生追悼論文集 (East and West: Essays
in Honor of Professor Maejima Shinji), ed. Keiō gijuku daigaku
Tōyō shi kenkyūshitsu 慶應義塾大学東洋史研究室
(Keiō University, Department of East Asian History), Tokyo,
Kyūko shoin, 1985.

Nishijima:

Nishijima Sadao hakase kanreki kinen: Higashi Ajia shi ni okeru
kokka to nōmin 西嶋定男博士還暦記念:東アジア史に
おける国家と農民 (Commemorating the 60th Birthday of
Professor Nishijima Sadao: The State and the Peasantry in East
Asian History), Tokyo, Yamakawa shuppansha, 1984.

Okamoto:

Ajia shominzoku ni okeru shakai to bunka: Okamoto Keiji sensei
taikan kinen ronshū アジア諸民族における社会と文化：岡本
敬二先生退官記念論集 (Society and Culture Among the
Peoples of Asia: Essays Commemorating the Retirement of
Professor Okamoto Keiji), Tokyo, Kokusho kankōkai, 1984.

Ran no kōzu:

Chūgoku shi ni okeru ran no kōzu 中国史における乱の構図
(The Structure of Rebellions in Chinese History), ed. Noguchi
Tetsurō 野口鉄郎, Tokyo, Yūzankaku, 1986.

Sakuma:

Sakuma Shigeo kyōju taikyū kinen Chūgoku shi tōji ronshū 佐久
間重男教授退休記念中国史・陶磁論集 (Essays on
Chinese History and Pottery in Commemoration of the Retirement
of Professor Sakuma Shigeo), Tokyo, Ryōgen shoten, 1983.

Sanshigyō:

Chūgoku sanshigyō no shi teki tenkai 中国蚕糸業の史的展開
(The Historical Development of the Sericulture Industry in
China), ed. Steering Committee for the Symposium on Modern and
Contemporary Chinese Economic History, Tokyo, Kyūko shoin, 1986.

Satō:

Satō hakase taikan kinen Chūgoku suirishi ronsō 佐藤博士
退官記念,中国水利史論叢 (Commemorating the Retire-
ment of Professor Satō: Essays on the History of Water Control
in China), Tokyo Kokusho kankōkai, 1984.

Shakai:

Shakai keizai shigaku no kadai to tembō 社会経済史学の課
題と展開 (Themes and Prospects in the Study of Social and
Economic History), ed. Shakai keizai shigakkai 社会経済史
学会 , Tokyo, Yūhikaku, 1984.

Taga:

Ajia no kyōiku to shakai: Taga Akigorō hakase koki kinen
ronbunshū アジアの教育と社会：多賀秋五郎博士古稀
記念論文集 (Education and Society in Asia: Essays
Commemorating the 70th Birthday of Professor Taga Akigorō),
Tokyo, Fushōdō, 1983.

Tanaka:

Chūgoku kindai shi no shomondai: Tanaka Masayoshi sensei taikan
kinen ronshū 中国近代史の諸問題：田中正美先生退官
記念論集 (Problems in the Modern History of China: Essays
Commemorating the Retirement of Professor Tanaka Masayoshi),
Tokyo, Kokusho kankōkai, 1984.

Glossary

Abe Takeo 安信健夫
aiguobu 愛国布
Anle 安樂
Anliang 安良
Ansei 安政
baila 白拉
Banzai Rihachirō
坂西利八郎
baojia 保甲
baolan 包攬
Baoquan 宝卷
beidonggu 備東穀
Beiyang 北洋
Benguan 本貫
"Bianshen lun" 編審論
caimai 採買
cang 倉
Changde 常德
changlao 長老
Chen Baozhen 陳宝箴
Chen Meng 岑猛
Chen Xiongfan 陳雄藩

Chen Zilong 陳子龍
cheng 城
chengjia 承佃
chiiki shakai 地域社会
Chongan xian zhi 崇安県志
chouzhuang 綱莊
Chūgoku nōson kankō chōsa
中国農村慣行調査
chūshin bubun 中心部分
Dai Zhen 戴震
Dali 大理
danhu 蛋户
danmin 蛋民
Dazu 大足
dangweixing 当為性
"Daoqi" 道器
dayi 大役
ding 丁
dingshou 頂首
Donglin 東林
duyushi 都御史

Duan Qirui 段祺瑞

Fangsheng hui 放生会

Fei Yucheng 費玉成

fenyu 分圩

Feng Guifen 馮桂芬

Fenghua 奉化

fengjian 封建

Foshan 仏山

fumin 富民

Funan 阜南

Furen zazhi 婦人雜誌

Fushe 復社

Fu Yiling 傅衣凌

Gelaohui 哥老会

Gezhi 格致

Gezhi huipian 格致彙編

gongsheng 貢生

gongsuo 公所

Gongyang 公羊

gongyi 公議

guan 官

guantian 官田

guanye 管業

Guanyin 観音

guanggun 光棍

guiji 詭寄

Guiping 桂平

guotou 過投

guotouyin 過投銀

Hainan 海南

hang 行

Hankou 漢口

haozu 豪族

Hitotsubashi 一橋

Honglou meng 紅楼夢

Huang 黄

Huang Liuhong 黄六鴻

Huangshan 黄山

Huang Tizheng 黄体正

Huang Zunxian 黄遵憲

Huang Xing 黄興

Huizhou 徽州

huogeng shuinou 火耕水耨

Iming futu hui 一命浮図会

Imjo 仁朝

Jiali 嘉礼

jiansheng 監生

Jiang Di 江地

Jiang Dunfu 蔣敦復
Jiang Yingjia 姜応甲
Jiang-Zhe 江浙
"Jiaoyang" 教養
Jingui 金匱
Jinhua 金華
Jinpingmei 金瓶梅
jinshi 進士
Jinxiang 金鄉
Jiusheng chuan 救生船
Jōshū 上州
junbuju 浚浦局
juren 擧人
jushi 局士
juanjian 捐監
Kang Jae-on 姜在彦
Kang Youwei 康有為
kaocheng fa 考成法
kejia 客家
kemin 客民
Kitamura 北村
Kobayashi Yoshihiro 小林義広
Kōbe 神戸
Kojima Kazuo 古島和雄
kong 空

Kuaihuo 快
kuisong 餽送
kyōdōtai 共同体
kyōshin ron 郷紳論
laohu 老戸
Leyun 樂雲
Lidai baoan 歴代宝案
Li Dazhao 李大釗
Li Hongzhang 李鴻章
Li Shizeng 李石曹
Li Xiucheng 李秀成
Li Wenzhi 李文治
Li Zicheng 李自成
lijia 里甲
lilaoren 里老人
liyuan 吏員
lizhang 里長
Liang Shiyi 梁士詒
Liang Qichao 梁啓超
Liang Tingnan 梁廷枬
liangzhang 糧長
Liaodong 遼東
linghu 另戸
linghu (broker) 領戸
Liu Ao 劉璈

Liu Kunyi 劉坤一

Liuliu-Liuqi 劉六劉七

Liu Mingchuan 劉銘伝

Liuyang 瀏陽

Longhu 龍虎

louqui 陋規

Lou Jinyuan 婁近垣

Lu Xun 魯迅

Lu Zhengxiang 陸徴祥

Lu Zhuangzhang

盧贛章

Luo 羅

Luo Xianglin 羅香林

maijia 買價

Mao Zedong 毛沢東

Maruyama Matsuyuki 丸山松幸

Miyun 密雲

min 民

minzu 民族

Mingxue 名学

Ming shilu 明実録

Ming Taizu 明太祖

Nakasone 中曽根

Nanhai 南海

nanbei juan 南北巻

nanbeizhong juan 南北中巻

Nangong 南贛

Nantong 南通

Nanxuehui 南学会

neidachen 内大臣

neiwufu zongguan

内務府総官

Nian 捻

Niida Noboru 仁井田陞

Nishijima Sadao 西嶋定男

Nishi Junzō 西順蔵

nubian 奴変

nupu 奴僕

pu 舗

Puji tang 普済堂

Qi Biaojia 祁彪佳

qilao 耆老

Qishan 琦善

qianzhuang 銭荘

Qiao Jishi 喬済時

Qinyong 勤勇

qing 頃

Qufu 曲阜

Quzhou 衢州

ren 仁

Sakatani Yoshirō 阪谷芳郎

sanshi 三世

Sanshi nian riji
三十年日記

Sen Ge 森各

Shanhua 善化

shanjuan 善捐

shanren 善人

shanshi 善士

Shantou 汕頭

Shang Bazhi 尚巴志

Shang Zhen 尚真

Shaoxing 紹興

sheren 舍人

Shenbao 申報

Shengshi weiyan 盛世危言

Shengzezhen 盛沢鎮

shengyuan 生員

shenshi 紳士

Shi Dakai 石達開

Shigeta Atsushi 重田德

shiji 市集

Shuntian 順天

Songjiang 松江

Song Zejiu 宋則久

Suzhou 蘇

Sun Jinbiao 孫金彪

Sun Zhongshan 孫中山

Taiping tianguo guanxi
lunwen mulu biao
太平天国関係論文目録表

Taiyuan 太原

Tan Sitong 譚嗣同

Tangkouzhen 湯口鎮

ti 体

tidu 提督

tidujunwu 提督軍務

tiyong 体用

Tiandi 天地

Tianming 天命

Tianyan lun 天演論

tianxia 天下

Tongmenghui 同盟会

Tongshan hui 同善会

Tongzhou 通州

Tsun-wan yat-bo 循環日報

tuhao 土豪

tujia 図甲

tusi 土司

tuanlian 団練

Wang Fuzhi 王夫之

Wang Gen 王艮

Wang Jingwei 汪精衛

Wang Tao 王韜

Wang Xinzhai 王心斎

Wang Yangming 王陽明

wei 衛

weitian 囲田

Wei Yuan 魏源

weixuanfu 衛選簿

wen 文

wulai 無頼

Wu Zhihui 呉稚暉

Xianfeng Tongzhi nian zuce
咸豐同治年図冊

xiangshen 郷紳

Xiangyang 襄陽

xiangyue 郷約

Xiao Chaogui 蕭朝貴

Xie Fucheng 薛福成

xin 心

Xin'an 新安

Xin qingnian 新青年

Xizou 息陬

Xu Du 許都

xuli 胥吏

Xuli hui 恤嫠会

Xu Peiyuan 徐佩瑗

Xu Shou 徐壽

xue 学

xunfu 巡撫

Xunzi 荀子

Yamakawa Kikue 山川菊栄

Yan Fu 嚴復

Yan'ge hui 掩骼会

yanlu 言路

Yang Guozhen 楊国楨

Yang Sichang 楊嗣昌

yangwu 洋務

yangwu pai 洋務派

Yang Xiuqing 楊秀清

Yao Tinglin 姚廷遴

Yasukuni 靖国

yazu 押租

ye 業

Ye 葉

Yin 鄞

Yining 義寧

Yishan 奕山

yitian liangzhu 一田兩主

yong 用

Yongan wen bieji
康盦文別集

Yongding 永定

youmin 遊民

Yuan dianzhang 元典章

Yuanhe 元和

Yuan Shikai 袁世凱

Yulin tuce 魚鱗圖冊

yutian 圩田

Yuying tang 育嬰堂

yuezhang 約長

Zai Tianchou 載天仇

Zhang Zhidong 張之洞

zhangfang 丈放

Zhanghua 彰化

Zhang Luoxing 張洛行

Zhang Shicheng 張士誠

Zhang Shusheng 張樹聲

Zhang Weiren 張偉仁

Zhang Zaigong 張再公

zhen 鎮

zhenshou 鎮守

Zheng Guanying 鄭觀応

zhengke 徵課

Zheng Qin 鄭欽

Zheng Zhu 鄭銖

zhi 職

zhi (substance) 質

Zhixin mianbing fa
治心免病法

zhobo 酌撥

Zhonghua gemingdang
中華革命黨

Zhongshan 中山

Zhongxue 中學

Zhongyi 忠義

Zhuji 諸暨

zhusheng 諸生

Zhu Xi 朱熹

Zhu Yuanzhang 朱元璋

Zhunyu lunke jiyao
準玉輪科輯要

Zizai 自在

zongguan 総管

Zuo Guangxian 左光先

Zuo Zongtang 左宗棠